London Trolleybus Depots Part Two

1707 has run into Hammersmith depot for the last time as it is the evening of Tuesday 19th July 1960; her final journey was as the last 626 from Clapham Junction. A ferry crew are taking her to Edmonton depot where she will have another nine months' service – whether the blinds were altered on this long trip is not known. The boy with a satchel on his back is the author.

Hugh Taylor

Published by Adam Gordon

D2 441 is on Bexleyheath depot forecourt and adjacent to a 'dolly stop' which states 'PARK UNDER WIRE'. Possibly this is a temporary stand for Bexleyheath Market Place due to it being unavailable for some reason. 698s would have to be 'trolleyed' into the depot to park where 441 is situated. Passengers would transfer to buses on routes 122 and 229 for the town centre. In the background is RT 491 on route 122. *John L. Smith*

Amendments to Part 1

Page	3	The reference to 1671 should read 'twin steering across the front twin axles.' It also had four rear road wheels, making it the only trolleybus in the fleet to have eight wheels.
Page	59	The top photograph is of 470B not 407B.
Page	61	Charlton manufactured trolleybus blinds until early 1952 not early 1951. Chiswick Works also produced 'paper' blinds for Hammersmith Depot.
Page	62	The conductor of 151 has changed the destination blind early and 151 is still on its way to Hounslow; therefore it will pass Chiswick Works on the way back.
Page	110	The photograph is taken in Blackhorse Lane not Blackhorse Road.
Page	114	Top photo: 1153 is travelling south, the driver having failed to change the destination blind from its starting point - Chingford Mount.
Page	117	Becontree Avenue should read Beacontree Avenue.
Page	153	There are differences in the capacity table to those quoted at the projected trolleybus depots. It was often the case that there was more than one estimation for many projects.

Copyright Hugh Taylor 2018. All rights reserved. No part of this publication may be reproduced, stored in a retrieval system or transmitted in any form or by any means, electronic, mechanical, photocopying, recording or otherwise without the prior permission in writing from the author.

ISBN 978-1-910654-16-3

Publication no.120

Published in 2018 by Adam Gordon, Kintradwell Farmhouse, Brora, Sutherland, KW9 6LU
Tel: 01408 622660   E-mail: adam@ahg-books.com

Designed and typeset by Barnabas Gordon
Tel: 07795 201 502   Email: Barney@ahgbooks.com

Printed by Henry Ling Limited, at the Dorset Press, Dorchester, DT1 1HD

AUTHOR'S NOTE
TEARING THROUGH THE NIGHT

The primary school I attended in Edgware was right outside the 664 trolleybus terminus; additionally 645s passed by on their roundabout journey from Canons Park to Barnet. In rush hours, 666s were also on the scene. Trolleybuses, with their booms, electric sparks and overhead, held far more fascination for me than the motorbus. Bus spotting had started in 1952 and was mainly local. With the advent of Red Rovers on 12th October 1957 my geographical sphere was greatly enhanced; the first day of these tickets saw me over at the East End where Poplar and West Ham were still using punch, rack and tickets; it was also Ilford's last day using this system of fare collection.

As stated in my Author's note in Part One I made a niche at Isleworth depot; however, it was 47 years before anybody asked 'Why Isleworth when Colindale was just down the road?' That was Adrian O'Callaghan who was third last to qualify as a London trolleybus driver. This is how it goes.

With the trolleybus to bus conversion imminent, I thought it best to follow the outgoing mode of transport rather than the incoming one. When stage six came round (April 1960) I spent the last day with the 687/697/699; it was just at the end of the Easter school holidays. Attending for some of the time on last days occurred henceforth; could be half day or full day - just bunked off school. Seeing in the last one at various depots was now my aim. By the time it got to stage eleven it was de rigueur; this was Tuesday 18th July 1961 and embraced Edmonton and Stamford Hill depots. Enquiries led to the information that the last one of this stage was a 643 from Holborn Circus which was due into Stamford Hill depot at 12.56am – this was trolleybus 1216 on SF 12. In the evening it was changed over for 1326. I boarded the vehicle at Stamford Hill and travelled to Wood Green and then Holborn Circus. Heading back to the depot, the driver went through a section insulator in Old Street at full speed causing an enormous flash in the darkness. Stamford Hill depot was reached and now I had to get home. Parked in Egerton Road was 1335 whose crew, I later found out, were waiting for 1326 so they could travel to Fulwell together. Now, last one in would be last one out so I waited at the exit for 1326 to appear. I got on and asked the crew if they would give me a lift to Cricklewood. The reply was "Do you know the way?" I answered in the affirmative. They hadn't been over to this part of London before; the driver was from Fulwell and the guard from Isleworth. They replied "Get under the staircase until we're out of sight of the depot." 1335 had left by now. There was no frog to pull at the end of Egerton Road but when we got to Bruce Grove I pulled the semi-automatic frog so they could proceed to Wood Green. At that point, 1238 passed the other way showing 649 AMHURST PARK STAMFORD HILL. I didn't know what was going on but it turned out to be Edmonton's staff trolleybus which didn't get in until well after 2a.m. However I'd made my choice and it was as well, because the last few Edmonton vehicles weren't taken away until Wednesday and Thursday.

1326's driver was in unfamiliar territory; his thinking was that the sooner they were back to Fulwell, the sooner they'd be home. Tearing through the night he was unaware of a section breaker in Lordship Lane and went through it at full speed. There was a sudden 'oomph' and 1326 lost power. Simultaneously there was an almighty banging and crashing from above. Dewirement. Bearing in mind the flashing of 1326 in Old Street it is assumed that probably all of Stamford Hill's vehicles hadn't had their trolley head carbons inspected on Monday night. The noise caused lights to go on in front bedroom windows of a number of houses both sides of the road. Amazingly, despite 1326's speed, there was no damage to the booms or overhead – fortunately there was a bamboo pole beneath the vehicle and the guard put the poles back on the wires. I photographed him doing this. We got to the end of Lordship Lane and I pulled the frog handle down for Jolly Butchers Hill; passing Wood Green depot I pulled a frog handle again so 1326 could go into Bounds Green Road. Here, we noticed 1335 on 641 wires going towards Winchmore Hill; the crew had no idea of where to go and 1335 was making an escape from Valhalla; it was reversed back over the junction and we waited for it to come up behind. At Kingsway, North Finchley I transferred 1326's booms to the

Cricklewood-bound wires - 1335's crew did likewise. At the bottom of Cricklewood Lane I pulled the semi-automatic frog handle for Hammersmith for 1326 – as soon as it was over the points I pulled it again for 1335. The crew of 1326 said they knew the way from there; they must have taken withdrawn trolleybuses to Colindale. Now, they're both off to Fulwell – later than planned. I walked towards Edgware but on the way an RF staff bus which had been taking ferry crews home, gave me a lift.

Stage twelve occurs. Stage thirteen occurs – these are my local routes. For the last two days (1st and 2nd January 1962) I spent the whole time travelling and appreciating what would be lost forever. It was biting cold but I was not going to miss a moment. Last in was 1666 at Stonebridge. Lift home again, this time by a fellow enthusiast. The following Saturday, 6th January, I was over on the Fulwell and Isleworth routes. I took with me a picture of the Isleworth guard rewiring 1326. Nightfall saw me at Isleworth and I showed the maintenance staff on duty the photograph. As explained in Part One they invited me in that day; I saw 1326's guard the following Saturday and he was grateful for the picture. From now on I had the run of IH. The 657 route required twenty two vehicles on a Saturday; the service was cut down in the evening and it dropped from a four minute headway to one every seven or eight minutes. At this time of day they all ran in from Hounslow and almost invariably 'the depot 657' would be right behind the 'through 657'. Ten for the depot, twelve for 'The Bush'. I would be at the frog and as soon as the 'through bus' passed over the points, I would pull the frog handle down. Driver and conductor would acknowledge with a wave as they didn't have to stop. It was all very slick and it must have looked 'hairy' to anyone watching from the other side of the road - the 657 didn't stop and the trolley arms would suddenly move at speed to the right. Crews had every confidence in me and there was never a dewirement; the booms did sway a bit but the drivers knew their overhead. As soon as the 657 was in the depot, I grabbed a bamboo and dropped the poles; one of the maintenance men would then battery manoeuvre the vehicle into the parking area.

The five maintenance staff, who are named in Part One, were very accommodating as were most of the crews. Many men, when asked what took them from boyhood to manhood, would reply by saying that there was a woman involved! For me it was the Isleworth trolleybusmen and their twenty six K1 class trolleybuses. I now name a number of the platform staff: Tony Shanny, Terry Shaw, Adrian O'Callaghan, Clarrie White, George Merry, Bert Barlow, George Legge, Les Lumley, Malcolm Parris, Bruce Henderson, Titch Truman, Percy Abeyasekera, P.J. Moran, Sonny Oxley, Joe Brew, Jim Collaghan, Sam East, Roy Bishop, Feidlim McLoughlin and Alan Buckland. There were three conductresses I remember: Ena Down, Phyllis Constable and Edith Scott. Thank you all for your kindness. I was very intrigued by a last driving school starting in February and the consequent passing out of three Isleworth conductors to drivers. Last to pass was Terry Shaw; he confirmed almost half a century later what I knew, when he said "We liked having you there". I wasn't just interested in the vehicles but also in the staff and their stories – hence his comment.

One of the maintenance staff was particularly kind – Ron Hayward. His last day of work at the depot was Monday 7th May; I boarded 1116 that evening to Hounslow terminus and bought a packet of ten Woodbine cigarettes. Returning on the same vehicle I gave them to Ron and thanked him for accommodating me. He did turn up on 8th May as he said he wasn't going to let his depot close without seeing it that day. His new location was Twickenham Bus Garage and I did make an attempt to see him there one Saturday but to no avail. Many years later, at Fulwell, I asked about him. A member of the maintenance staff said he'd worked there until quite recently but had now retired; however, he came up to the depot from time to time – I asked them to tell him that the youngster who helped him with trolley booms at Isleworth, and was now a bus driver with London Transport, was asking after him. Sometime later, a mechanic who had worked with him at FW knew his address. I got hold of his phone number and dialled it; his wife picked up the receiver. I asked if Ron was there and she asked who it was; I told her. She said he'd died three months previously. There is no other emotion I've ever experienced greater than that of disappointment. I did go and see his widow and granddaughter and produced photographs of him at work. He'll never know how he affected my life; if it hadn't been for him it may not have taken the direction it did. All down to 1326 though, with its driver 'tearing through the night'.

ACKNOWLEDGEMENTS

The original idea was for 'London Trolleybus Depots' to be in three parts. That has proved impractical both in the terms of keeping the books at affordable prices and to use photographs to their best effect; that means continuing house-style of either one or two images to a page. Consequently the subject will be in four parts. I considered it parochial to confine the book to just the depot itself so have taken a wider approach and included the routes and environs worked by each depot; included is a picture on each of their main services.

Tony Belton, Ken Blacker, Jim Hawkins, Fred Ivey and Charlie Wyatt have checked the draft. I never thought that I would meet a member of staff who worked at Bexleyheath depot but a chance meeting by Wendy Davis (wife of Peter Davis who bought London tram 1858) with Jean Cole who was a conductress there led to her relating her experiences on trolleybuses. Jean's story is in her own words; the author has provided the insider information and in conjunction with her has prepared the captions. John Carwardine provided the destination blind facsimiles; all are from genuine blinds unless otherwise stated. Tony Belton has scanned many negatives and Barney Gordon has been responsible for the layout. Roger Smith has provided the map of the system. Wife Catherine ('er indoors) has typed the draft and her time spent on this is appreciated. All photographs attributed to 'London Transport Museum' are credited to ©TfL from the London Transport Museum Collection. Bill Haynes views are used with the permission of the Tramway & Light Railway Society. A map of the overhead layout of each depot is provided.

I recommend readers to the London Trolleybus website at www.trolleybus.net which is an excellent forum for enthusiasts. If any reader wants to communicate with me and has any additional information or photographs about this subject or wishes to enter into dialogue with me please do so at isleworthdepot@trolleybus.net.

It is 1.30am on Wednesday 19th July 1961 in Lordship Lane. The Fulwell driver hit a section breaker at speed with the trolley arms flying all over the place. Amazingly there was no damage to the booms and overhead. The Isleworth guard rewires 1326. *Hugh Taylor*

It is now 2am at Cricklewood Broadway on Wednesday 19th July 1961 and 1326 with 1335 behind, take the semi-automatic frog at the bottom of Cricklewood Lane to speed them on their way to Fulwell Works. *Hugh Taylor*

ISLEWORTH TROLLEYBUSMEN

It is Saturday 9th March 1962 and Ron Hayward rests his right hand on 1060, a trolleybus that he helped to look after for about a year. The working environment was so clean at Isleworth depot that he usually worked in his 'civvies'. *Hugh Taylor*

The highest numbered driver's Metropolitan Stage Carriage Licence Badge was issued to an Isleworth man. This was Adrian O'Callaghan who was given T14898. Adrian is seen on 19th April 1962 with trolleybus 1113 and conductor Chandra at the 657 terminus at Hounslow. London Transport were often tardy getting uniform to staff but were quick off the mark in issuing Adrian a brand new driver's dustcoat. *Hugh Taylor*

Driver Clarrie White and conductor Feidlim McLoughlin were typical rank and file of the London trolleybus fleet. They were amongst a number of staff who accommodated my interest. 1114 is at the Hounslow terminus on 7th April 1962; note that the painter has put the IH code in the wrong position on the nearside and 1114 is running as 12 IH. After he had finished work on 8th May, Feidlim said he wasn't going to work on motorbuses and was packing it up that night. He gave me his MSC badge which is illustrated below. Clarrie only dewired once during his long trolleybus career. This occurred when driving a Q1 and he had to slam on his brakes to avoid a child who ran into the road. The sudden movement of the vehicle caused the booms to come off the wires. *Hugh Taylor*

Jack Guy, in dirty overalls, stands on the offside of 1060 during the evening of Saturday 9th March 1962. One evening he took me into the cab of one of the K1s and showed me how trolleybuses operated by battery and trolley. *Hugh Taylor*

BEXLEYHEATH

Opened 10th November 1935 and the only new trolleybus depot. There was much discontent from local residents who said it was being built in a residential area without prior consultation; objections were overcome but 'locals' continued to bombard London Transport about the noise factor. Staff were instructed not to leave motor generator sets running unnecessarily. In March 1937 an area in the depot was set aside for giving 'partial' overhauls to its own vehicles prior to Charlton Works taking on this work in early 1938. Bendix brake test equipment was available on one pit. A bomb hit the depot on 7th November 1940; thirty-seven vehicles were damaged with four requiring new bodies. At 3.12am on 29th June 1944 the building received a direct hit; twelve vehicles were destroyed and twenty six needed re-bodying – thirty nine were damaged, some severely. Amazingly, seven of the eighty-four were unscathed. London Transport describe the incident as 'building on fire, depot wiped out - no trolleybuses fit for service' - an exaggeration. Despite this, an almost full service was achieved that evening by drafting in vehicles from all over the system; on page 204 is a list made by a member of staff who had the presence of mind to record those arriving then and in the ensuing weeks.

As part of the South London tram conversion scheme, route 698 was to be extended to Eltham; to accommodate extra vehicles the depot was to be extended by forty eight feet, taking the capacity to 105. This would have been achieved by building out on the turning circle at the rear; the concept did not come to fruition. There was a wiring circuit for driver training - it was also used to see who could hold the lap record!

Closed to trolleybuses on 3rd March 1959.
Routes operated: 694, 696, 698.
Type used: Leyland.
Capacity under cover was 75.
Number of vehicles allocated in March 1951 was 86.
Last trolleybus into depot - 405B on route 698.

A number of the new trolleybus drivers and conductors at Bexleyheath depot pose for the photographer - they have presented themselves immaculately. Drivers and conductors had to wear white coats and caps between April 1st and October 31st; at other times they had to wear serge navy blue coats and caps. As some are wearing serge coats, the exact date of this view taken in 1936 cannot be ascertained. Only a few display their licence badges; officialdom was strict on this matter so there was a slip-up here. Three inspectors and someone who may be the District Superintendent have got themselves into the photograph. Four B2s are in the background with only 123 being identifiable.

Pennyfare Magazine, courtesy Bexleyheath Local Studies & Archive Centre

On 7th August 1935 the future Bexleyheath trolleybus depot is little more than a shell. The construction firm (J. Jarvis & Sons) worked at great speed to enable opening to occur on 10th November that year. Scaffolding is wooden with workmen concentrating their efforts on the office block. *London Transport Museum U18101*

Taken on the same day as the previous view concrete has been laid, allowing traction poles to be placed at the rear of the site. Those in the centre, and on the left, have concrete surrounds to their bases; they will be painted white in wartime to indicate their position to staff. The traction pole on the immediate right has its base enclosed in wooden shuttering; presumably it is holding wet concrete in position. The other poles aligned with it will receive the same treatment in due course. Finials have yet to be fitted to the top of the poles; two overhead tracks are in position. *London Transport Museum U18100*

The builders continue with their work in November 1935; inside the depot a few vehicles are parked. The doors are still in primer but will be painted green in due course; circular casks on the forecourt hold reels of copper overhead wire to be erected locally. The road surface in Erith Road is in an appalling condition and was a contributing factor for trams in the area being early candidates for conversion to trolleybuses. For training purposes, wiring leads from the Belvedere direction directly into the depot; this facility was removed during the war. Thereafter all 698s travelled to Bexleyheath Market Place before returning to the depot.

London Transport Museum U18889

Taken from the opposite direction on the same day, wooden boundary posts are being fitted. Very noticeable is the fact that all traction standards do not have finials; this will have to be dealt with quickly to prevent rain entering. Both photographs on this page show the appalling state of the track on which trams on route 98 are still running. Passengers are in for a bumpy ride.

London Transport Museum 18888

These two photos feature the opening of the 'Bexley system' and the second stage of the tram to trolleybus conversion; a number of London Transport bigwigs and local dignitaries are at the depot entrance as a gleaming B2 96 stands on the forecourt. They will travel on 96 to Woolwich from where a Green Line coach will take them to 'The Bull', Dartford where luncheon will be served (they are unable to travel by trolleybus as the wiring is not complete at Welling). This is conversion day, 10th November 1935, and the 698 service has been working for a few hours. B2 103 has been out on the road and approaches the end of its journey to Bexleyheath Market Place. 96 appropriately shows 698 SPECIAL - the route plate for the same service is adjacent to the conductor's signalling window. Advertisements were fitted either side of the rear destination and route boxes at this time; however, London Transport have blacked out the rear adverts on these vehicles which were for John Bull whisky. The photographs are so sharp that 96's budget holes to open up the rear blind box are easily observed. Bystanders marvel at the new era.

London Transport Museum U18906/18907

The first trolleybus to arrive at Bexleyheath depot was prototype X3 63 – it was one of two vehicles trialled as the standard London trolleybus. As a four-wheeler it came second to the six wheeler (No 62) which at thirty feet in length was deemed more suitable for the capital. The wires are energised in the depot and 63 will be used for driver training both here and in the locality. The original front route and destination boxes have already been altered; it would go through one more change in later years. The side box has a Fulwell blind fitted. Work progresses on the depot. This view and the one below are at the rear of the depot.

Glazing has yet to be fitted to the depot doors. The overhead layout is still being assembled as many span wires hang loosely. Construction staff will have to get a move on as it is opening month - November 1935. Crossing from left to right is the training circuit; bracket arms are temporary and will be removed in due course. Trolleybus 115 stands with its poles down - blinds are yet to be fitted so it is a very recent delivery.

London Transport Museum U18884

Bexleyheath was London Transport's only purpose-built trolleybus depot and an impressive sight with its wide modern frontage and rows of vehicles lined-up purposefully inside. This view was taken on 9th May 1936 shortly after permission was received to run thirty foot trolleybuses on the Bexley area routes to cope with unexpectedly high passenger demand. The vehicle standing just behind the white coated driver is C1 174, one of the AECs recently transferred in to provide additional capacity. All others are 'native' B2 class Leylands as is 126 passing by on the 698 whose conductor has already changed the front destination blind in readiness for its next return journey. It is fortunate that it is a dry day as 126's offside windscreen wiper is missing!

Alfred Monk, courtesy Roger Monk

Bexleyheath tram depot is seen between the LPTB takeover of London's tramways and the start of trolleybus services in the Bexley area. These premises were too small and therefore unsuitable to adapt for the new trolleybus services. In view is an ex-LCC M class car; these replaced decrepit trams formerly working in the locality. A couple of ancillary vehicles can be seen. Erith tram depot was closed at the same time as Bexleyheath tram depot. Felix the depot cat was a good 'mouser' here and was transferred to Bexleyheath trolleybus depot and made an honorary member of the Transport and General Workers Union on account of keeping down any vermin that were inclined to visit the new premises.

N.D.W. Elston

What a difference between the new trolleybus depot and the old tram depot. Just a year after trolleybuses were introduced to the area, Bexleyheath depot is seen from Erith Road. There is no doubt who the building belongs to - LONDON TRANSPORT; a 'Bexleyheath Depot' sign was never placed alongside. This view on 30th December 1936 shows a number of B2s with a C1 on the right. Parked on the far left is an LT type bus on route 122; the wiring by the office block is part of the circuit that enabled trainees to gain the feel of a trolleybus without having to venture on to the public highway. Tram track has been removed although the road surface leaves much to be desired. The surrounds at the base of the traction poles are concrete. During the war they were painted white to assist staff in the blackout. See top of page 206.

London Transport Museum U22386

Bexleyheath was London Transport's only purpose-built trolleybus depot and an impressive sight with its wide modern frontage and rows of vehicles lined-up purposefully inside. This view was taken on 9th May 1936 shortly after permission was received to run thirty foot trolleybuses on the Bexley area routes to cope with unexpectedly high passenger demand. The vehicle standing just behind the white coated driver is C1 174, one of the AECs recently transferred in to provide additional capacity. All others are 'native' B2 class Leylands as is 126 passing by on the 698 whose conductor has already changed the front destination blind in readiness for its next return journey. It is fortunate that it is a dry day as 126's offside windscreen wiper is missing!

Alfred Monk, courtesy Roger Monk

Bexleyheath tram depot is seen between the LPTB takeover of London's tramways and the start of trolleybus services in the Bexley area. These premises were too small and therefore unsuitable to adapt for the new trolleybus services. In view is an ex-LCC M class car; these replaced decrepit trams formerly working in the locality. A couple of ancillary vehicles can be seen. Erith tram depot was closed at the same time as Bexleyheath tram depot. Felix the depot cat was a good 'mouser' here and was transferred to Bexleyheath trolleybus depot and made an honorary member of the Transport and General Workers Union on account of keeping down any vermin that were inclined to visit the new premises.

N.D.W. Elston

130, 114, 124 and 117 are in the maintenance area on 30th December 1936; although four pits exist there are just two sets of overhead so very precise shunting has taken place to ensure 114's trolleys do not foul 130's. When parking 114, a staff member may have shouted "That'll do" to its driver as there are only about six inches between trolley heads. 124 has its poles under its retaining hooks while its heads are attended to. All vehicles have been running on route 696; despite a BEXLEYHEATH DEPOT display being provided from the start of operations, all vehicles show BEXLEYHEATH MARKET PLACE. The route numerals are of a rounded style and were soon superseded by bolder ones. The vehicles advertise 'Bisto' beneath the rear window so maybe there is a block contract in place; 114 and 130 promote 'John Bull' magazine while 117 and 124 advertise Whitbread's ale and stout. Either this part of the depot or the next section across (which initially had brake-testing equipment) was used for overhauling Bexley's own vehicles before Charlton Works took on this task.   *London Transport Museum U22388*

The photographer is now at the front of the inspection area and captures not only the same four twenty-seven foot long B2s but also thirty foot long C1 179 on secondment from Fulwell until new D2s arrive. Vehicles are parked on raised pillars, giving staff easy access beneath and alongside vehicles; guard rails are an additional safety feature. Concrete buffers fitted to the end of the pillars prevent vehicles inadvertently rolling forward; it was not unknown for handbrakes to be left in the OFF position!

London Transport Museum U22389

What a difference between the new trolleybus depot and the old tram depot. Just a year after trolleybuses were introduced to the area, Bexleyheath depot is seen from Erith Road. There is no doubt who the building belongs to – LONDON TRANSPORT; a 'Bexleyheath Depot' sign was never placed alongside. This view on 30th December 1936 shows a number of B2s with a C1 on the right. Parked on the far left is an LT type bus on route 122; the wiring by the office block is part of the circuit that enabled trainees to gain the feel of a trolleybus without having to venture on to the public highway. Tram track has been removed although the road surface leaves much to be desired. The surrounds at the base of the traction poles are concrete. During the war they were painted white to assist staff in the blackout. See top of page 206.

London Transport Museum U22386

Bexleyheath depot on October 17th 1936 with the photograph taken to show the 50 watt PHILIPS 'Philora' sodium lamps equipped with ESLA Bi-Multi Reflectors; there were 57 which adequately lit the area. All vehicles are B2s of which the only identifiable one is 122; a TROLLEYBUS bulls-eye is next to its platform while above, a route plate complements the side blind. The main part of 122's roof is silver - the rear dome is red. The rear doors are unusually closed - the partition between the parking and pit areas is glass. In front of this a fire alarm bell can just be seen; the raised foreman's office is behind 122. A very important operational matter occurred here in the summer of 1939. Thirty of Bexley's sixty seater B2s moved to Holloway; replacing them were 32 seventy seater H1s; all came from Holloway. The H1s greater seating capacity was of far more use in an area gearing up for armament than on the quieter Hampstead routes. Bexleyheath ended up with 765, 766 and 784 to 813.

The first time the depot suffered major air raid damage, four vehicles needed re-bodying. One was H1 792 (on the left) photographed on 8th November 1940, the day after the attack. Much of the troughing is damaged and a sliding door hangs askew. Number 95 on the right is in a bad way; it will be re-bodied. 406 and 795 were the other vehicles sent away from here to Weymann's for re-bodying. *London Transport Museum U23580*

On the second occasion the depot was hit, 416 and 789 suffered extensive bodywork damage; however, both were repaired by London Transport. Not so fortunate was 435, in the centre, whose upper deck structure has disappeared; it remains with a number of others at the point of impact and will be 'written off'. For the Germans this was a lucky strike on 29th June 1944 as they could not predict where flying bombs would land; this photograph was taken that day. *London Transport Museum U35787*

An astonishing feat was performed when a fly-bomb hit Bexley trolleybus depot on 29th June, 1944. No fewer than 84 trolleybuses were damaged, a number being a total loss. But with the help of petrol buses and trolleybuses from other depots a practically normal service was operated *in the evening peak*.

The rear of the depot on 29th June 1944 sees 423, 451, 97, 401 and 94; they are not too severely damaged and will not need new bodies. The rear internal blind box housing of 401 hangs loosely. The overhead has survived but probably is not energised at present. A traction pole has number 8 chalked or painted onto it - maybe this indicated the road number in this difficult situation. *London Transport Museum U35790*

Seven women clear up after the near destruction of the depot on 29th June 1944; some appear happy to be in the photograph. Staff on tower wagon 6E are repairing overhead at the front of the depot; many of the staff have been called in on the day of the air strike to help out. The identity of the three trolleybuses in view is not known. Arthur Frederick Ansell Noyes was an electrician for London Transport. He assisted in wiring the new Bexleyheath depot in 1935; he was called back again to help re-wire the building in 1944 after extensive war damage. *London Transport Museum U35779*

Vehicles drafted in the aftermath of the 1944 air attack

Arrived 29th June

104 from Charlton Works	Stayed at Bexleyheath
410, 411, 434, 471, 472, 473 from West Ham	Stayed at Bexleyheath
467, 469 from Walthamstow	467 back to Walthamstow
	469 to Charlton Works
889, 890 893 from Edmonton	889 to West Ham Works
	890 back to Edmonton
	893 to Fulwell
971, 972, 973, 974 from Finchley	971 to Charlton Works
	972/973/974 to Fulwell Depot
1346 from Leyton	To West Ham
1406, 1407, 1527 from Poplar	To West Ham
1547, 1548, 1549, 1585 from Bow	1547/1548/1549 to West Ham
	1585 back to Bow
1702, 1703, 1704, 1711, 1712, 1720 from Holloway	1702/1703/1720 to Hammersmith
	1704/1711/1712 to Hanwell
608 from Charlton Works 30th June	Back to home depot – West Ham

Arrived 3rd July

609 from Charlton Works	Back to home depot – West Ham

Arrived 4th July

163 from Hounslow	To Fulwell
305, 306 from Finchley	To West Ham
465, 539 from Hammersmith	Back to Hammersmith
595 from Fulwell Works	Back to home depot – West Ham
850 from Wood Green	To Fulwell
1063, 1066 from Hanwell	Back to Hanwell
1097 from Stamford Hill	To Hanwell
1321 from Hackney	To West Ham
1528 from Poplar. Received war damage on 696 1.3.45	To West Ham

Arrived 7th September

637 from Charlton Works	Back to Charlton (7th May 1945)

Arrived 27th October

356 from Charlton Works	Back to home depot - Walthamstow

Arrived 1st November

327 from Hendon	To West Ham
329, 330 from Finchley	To West Ham
969 from Edmonton	To Fulwell
1061 from Hanwell	Back to Hanwell
1699 from Hammersmith	Back to Hammersmith

Arrived 8th November

593 from Fulwell Works	Back to home depot – West Ham
970 and 1524 recorded by PSV Circle	Presumably back to Finchley/West Ham

Five of Bexleyheath's own trolleybuses were away for overhaul at the time and survived the carnage. 388/399/438/785 were in Charlton Works, and 813 was in West Ham Works

London Transport have really shown their mettle as Edmonton's 893 has arrived as a reinforcement on 29th June; it is behind a K class vehicle with both available for service. A number blind is in the rear of 893 – maybe there are no more destination blinds available. On the left are some unidentified damaged vehicles.
London Transport Museum U24086

Good revenue was obtained through advertising on the sides of London Transport's vehicles; to promote this, trolleybuses were photographed at four depots and Charlton Works. On 2nd January 1948 On the instruction of London Transport, the first two vehicles from Northern Coachbuilders and the first four from East Lancs (i.e those delivered in 1945) were delivered minus one opening window on each side of the upper deck. The supplier of the opening windows was unable to produce enough of them because of shortages of material, and in preference to delaying the delivery of the six vehicles, London Transport instructed that they should be supplied with the centre half-drops on both sides of the upper deck replaced by fixed panes of glass.

A subsequent adjustment was made to the price paid for these bodies. 402C was the first to be delivered by Northern Coachbuilders. 402C's blind display is intriguing as BEXLEYHEATH is in large capitals while DEPOT is in small capitals. PICTURE POST took all the advert positions on this vehicle.
London Transport Museum U13924

It is 25th May 1954, seventeen and a half years after the photograph seen on page 200. Rebuilding saw the depot as almost the same design as before. As usual, some trolleybuses are out of service. Route 122 still uses the forecourt as a terminal point; RTL 210 has a latter day rear destination display while RTL 591 uses a reduced depth one. Most of the traction poles have white concrete surrounds; this enables staff to be more aware of them as London Transport has provided precious little lighting on the forecourt. The main means of illumination is a lamp shining onto Erith Road.
London Transport Museum U23830

The 'Running Shift' was responsible for much of the maintenance in the depots and for attending to failures, punctures and dewirements on the highway when they would take out a breakdown truck. There were two daytime shifts: 6am to 2pm and 2pm till 10pm which they worked alternately - the night shift had permanent staff. The number of men on duty at any one time during the day depended on the number of vehicles allocated to the depot.

The photographer visited depots on Sundays in the mid-fifties and it would appear that the full complement has turned out for him. There were about eighty-five vehicles allocated now which warranted four men – three have handed-down coats from drivers or conductors while one uses overalls. All are happy to pose in front of H1 798.
John L. Smith

"It's all over" as they say and Bexleyheath trolleybus depot is no more - it is 6th March 1959, three days into the first stage of the conversion programme. All but eight vehicles are going to Cohen's scrapyards at either Penhall Road, Charlton or Colindale; five of the doomed vehicles are in view. Nearest the camera is 415, then 390B, 473 and two others. All but one show BEXLEYHEATH DEPOT though in three different styles. There is a different advertisement on the back of each vehicle – their contracts finished on 3rd March 1959.

Alan Cross

VEHICLES OF INTEREST

One of the many vehicles sent to Bexleyheath in the aftermath of the 1944 attack was M1 1549 from Bow. 1549 has only worked as far as Abbey Wood on route 698; it shows the original destination display for this location. Having circled the loop here 1549 stands on the siding in Abeey Road. Wartime accoutrements: white paint has been applied to the front mudguards, shrouds have been positioned over the headlights and the side windows have anti-shatter netting. It must be summer as all the windows are open; Picture Post, which was published every Wednesday, is a striking advert. Adjacent to the cab is a recruitment poster for men and women conductors.

W. J. Haynes

Its sparkling condition implies that 107A has recently been overhauled. On what is obviously a hot day, both windscreens are partially open as are all top deck windows in view. Suffix A bodies were built with sliding ventilators as opposed to the usual half-drops. This vehicle, as short wheel-based B2 107, had its body destroyed while working from Holloway depot on 27th November 1940. It was one of sixteen re-bodied by Weymann; with its chassis lengthened it returned to London as D2A 107A. Due to the low grade material available at the time their bodies soon deteriorated and remedial work had to be carried out by Mann Egerton in 1949. On return from Weymann's, 107A was sent to West Ham; on 1st December 1952 it was transferred to Bexleyheath, staying in service until mid-1958. It was not until March 1959 that she was released for scrap. 107A is at Merewood Road, Barnehurst working on route 698 to Bexleyheath; the driver is changing the front blind, having forgotten to do this at his previous terminus. Turn to page 342 and see the plight of the vehicle there.

John L. Smith

Four East Lancs re-bodied trolleybuses returned without a half-drop window on each side of the top deck. One was 407B which is at Limewood Road, Northumberland Heath on 18th December 1954 on route 698. Note the pollarded trees and motorcyclist with sidecar. The Aldenham style route blind is 'out of sorts' with the Charlton destination blind. The other East Lancs vehicles to come back minus an opening window each side were 391B/392B and 409B. The London Transport rolling stock inspector kept in close touch with companies rebodying their trolleybuses and regularly visited their factories to ensure that their workmanship was of the highest standard. *Peter Mitchell 6636*

The trolleybuses rebodied by Northern Coachbuilders had a C suffix added to their fleet number. 430C is a very interesting vehicle. It was the second of two NCB vehicles delivered without a half-drop on each side of the top deck. It was later fitted with two extra half-drops, presumably at one of its overhauls. At Parsons Hill, Woolwich 430C on route 698 is outside The Castle pub; in half a minute it will be parked on the stand. Routes 694/696/698 were extended here from Woolwich Ferry in 1943. Consequently the traction poles between the two places had a number with a suffix; in view is C12. About a third of Bexley's trolleybuses were of the re-bodied variety in post-war years. *Alan Cross*

To conclude the Bexleyheath section, this view has been chosen to demonstrate the professionalism of the photographers that London Transport used. C1 157 is at Danson Park, Welling; the trolleybus is centred between the trees, and the post and chain fence. 157 has come from Hounslow depot and will spend about nine months operating on routes 696 and 698; as 157 will be in the area for some time it carries a WOOLWICH FOR SHOPPING advertisement. A number of C1s moved over from West London due to unpredicted passenger demand in the Bexley/Woolwich area following the tram to trolleybus conversion in the area. On 12th April 1936, C1 157 heads for WOOLWICH FERRY on route 696. Charlton Works would have had to carry out a rush job to supply blinds for all vehicles transferred in. *London Transport Museum U20100*

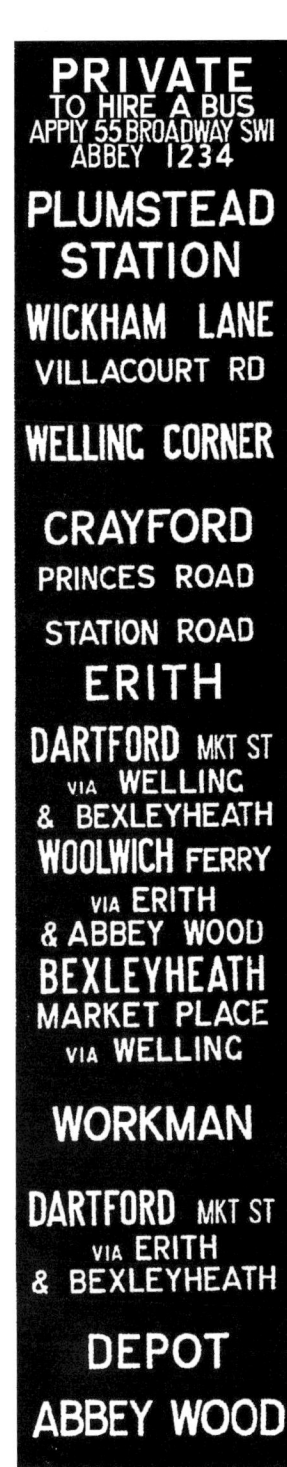

NOTES:
12-10-50: Woolwich Ferry is inappropriate as the terminus had been at Parsons Hill since 1943.
Clever use of words meant & BEXLEYHEATH DEPOT was one display, with DEPOT ABBEY WOOD being appropriate as trams still operated from that location at the time. The WORKMAN fares facility finished on 30th September 1950 but the blinds had already been ordered.
14-2-57 blind has a misspelling in that PRINCESS ROAD should read PRINCES ROAD.

LONDON TRANSPORT - CENTRAL ROAD SERVICES

Office of the Schedules Superintendent (R.T.),
55, Broadway, S.W.1.

31st December, 1958.

TO ALL CONCERNED

STAFF JOURNEYS - TROLLEYBUSES
(IN OPERATION WEEK COMMENCING 7TH JANUARY, 1959)

THIS RONEO IS IN ALPHABETICAL ORDER OF DEPOTS. THE ROUTE NUMBERS ADJACENT TO THE DEPOT NAME ARE THOSE UPON WHICH STAFF JOURNEYS OPERATE.

BEXLEY   ROUTES 696. 698

	Nights of Sunday/Monday to Friday/Saturday					Night of Saturday/Sunday					
	698	696	698	696	698	696	698	696	698	696	698	698
Dartford (Market Street)			12.37			4.19			12.37			
Princes Road						4.27						
Bexley Market Place		12.20	12.54	3. 0	4.30	4.36		12.20	12.54	3.27	4.41	4.49
Bexley Depot			12.59		4.35				12.59	3.32		
Bexley Market Place				3.11	4.48					3.45	4.52	5. 0
Erith (Wheatley Arms)					4.50							
Walnut Tree Road				3.26						3.59	5. 6	
Abbey Wood		12.29				4.45		12.29				
Welling Corner		12.42		3.36		4.59		12.42		4. 9		
Plumstead Station		12.44		3.37		5. 0		12.44		4.11		
Welling Corner		12.54		3.51		5.14		12.54		4.23	5. 8	
Abbey Wood					4.52							
Walnut Tree Road		1. 8		4. 0	4.54			1. 8				
Erith (Wheatley Arms)	12.14	1.21		4. 9	5. 7	5.23	12.14	1.21		4.32	5.22	5. 4
Bexley Depot						5.32				4.41	5.35	5.17
Bexley Market Place				4.17		5.40	12.31			4.49		
Princes Road	12.31											
Dartford (Market St.)		1.26						1.26			5.37	
Bexley Depot												

212

CARSHALTON (née Sutton)

Opened 8th December 1935. The only 'strike' during the war was on 5th July 1944 when blast damage saw seventeen trolleybuses with broken windows; all were repaired overnight and available for service next morning. The depot was never fully utilised and the generous space saw four withdrawn C2s stored here in the mid-1950s. In 1949 an idea floated when planning stage one of the tram conversion programme was for route 612 to be extended to West Croydon (for crew reliefs) and to be worked by Sutton depot. This did not occur but when Thornton Heath tram depot closed on 31st December 1949 its tower wagon came here. Re-named Carshalton on 12th July 1950.

Closed to trolleybuses on 3rd March 1959.
Routes operated: 630 (Christmas Day/Mitcham Fair; Summerstown on Coronation Day 1953), 654.
Type used: Leyland.
Capacity under cover was 51.
Number of vehicles allocated in March 1951 was 33.
Last trolleybus into depot: 83 - route 654.
The dates quoted for the opening of the depots are for the first full day of trolleybus operation. The closure date is the last full day of operation. Commencement dates of trams on these premises are not included as there are conflicting details; similarly details of the trolleybus depots as bus garages are not included as they are outside the scope of this book.

The South Metropolitan Electric Tramways sign fixed to the central pillar of the double arched entrance announces that this is their Sutton depot. Open top trams are used on service 7; a notice detailing cheap return fares on this route is positioned on one of the arches. A crew are about to enter the depot to take a tram out. Roads one to six are numbered; the doors on the right may be permanently closed. It is 30th August 1930.
London Transport Museum U7055

Seen in the depot's infancy, these views were taken in March and December 1936 respectively. The top one shows that tram track still exists in Benhill Avenue though it has been removed from the depot premises; concrete is laid to the boundary. LONDON TRANSPORT and SUTTON DEPOT signs have yet to be positioned on the administrative office. In the lower view the track has been removed and wiring alterations have taken place on the Croydon-bound overhead. A traffic recording impulse skate is now positioned on the positive wire; as each trolleybus head touched this device, a mark shows up on an instrument within the depot indicating the frequency of route 654. To take its extra weight more span wires have been erected; additional spans have been placed alongside the depot access wiring from Sutton. Trolleybuses entering the depot from Sutton require poles to be swung to a nearside set of wires. London Transport was miserly when it came to overhead equipment and would rather have men changing poles by hand than pay for a facing frog. In due course though, one would be installed.

London Transport Museum U19980/U22371

In this April 1936 view the brake tester, with its up-to-date equipment, is seen in the foreground. These machines were only fitted at a few depots and as Sutton was such a long way from any other, it was requisite for one to be installed here; it became redundant when road testing became normal practice. In the centre is the turntable/traverser which ran in a channel across the depot. Five trolleybuses are in view; one is over a docking pit. Beyond the traverser, 66, 71 and two others are parked. Bisto adverts are below the rear windows of 66 and 71; Bexley vehicles were similarly adorned. As can be seen, this is a very clean working environment. In the main yard, a tower wagon is just in view. *London Transport Museum U5748*

In April 1936, trolleybuses 88 and 74 are at the front of the depot - 74 shows SPECIAL. The three traction poles in view have spiked finials at the top; the centre standard holds a light to illuminate the forecourt.
London Transport Museum U5751

The office block at SUTTON DEPOT on 18th January 1951; renamed CARSHALTON DEPOT the previous July the London Transport Executive has yet to get its act together. The bottom three sets of windows are frosted; this prevents members of the public from looking in. A plaque bearing the words LONDON TRANSPORT HEAD OFFICE 55 BROADWAY WESTMINSTER SW1 is positioned on the office wall. The recording skate shown on page 214 has been removed - perhaps the 654 drivers' timekeeping obviated its use! The facing frog is now far nearer the entrance to the depot than in the views also on that page. *London Transport Museum U50826*

By the time the premises were photographed on 7th May 1954 CARSHALTON DEPOT is shown on the office block. During the war there was a lot of arcing and flashing when trolley booms were moved from one set of wires to another during blackout hours. This caused consternation in official quarters and consequently many regularly used layouts which had required trolley swings became frog operated; the one from Sutton is now operated by a handle on traction pole 475. To assist conductors during the blackout as to its position an oval white mark is painted on the standard; the mark is partly chipped away due to conductors, before pulling the handle down, giving two taps on it to signify that their drivers can go through the points and enter the depot. The building on the right houses the sub-station which states PRIVATE PUBLIC NOT ADMITTED. A panel for advertising purposes has been placed on the office building. *London Transport Museum U5319*

Sutton depot was re-named Carshalton depot in July 1950. Over its pits on 10th April 1955 are two resident B1s. Number 93, showing 654 CARSHALTON DEPOT, has Aldenham style blinds. Adjacent is 80 with Charlton blinds displaying 654 SUTTON DEPOT. It is almost five years since the change of name - the depot does not want to give up its original title. By now Carshalton had all thirty five short wheel-based B1s - 64 to 93, and 489 to 493, but not for much longer. Casual withdrawals of B1s commenced in May 1955 with others falling by the wayside in the ensuing years.

Wire greaser 114W is on Carshalton depot forecourt – it was not normally necessary to lubricate wires in depot confines but in this instance it seems to be happening. Behind is wagon 336V. *David Packer*

Corrugated iron above two bays has fallen into disrepair. The traction pole adjacent to the office block incorporates an overhead feeder - white bands on the standards signify this; two double white bands painted at the base of these standards are safety measures. The re-set skate on the positive wire was fitted subsequent to the commissioning of the depot and was the only example on the system of a semi-automatic frog inside depot premises; conductors push a button to operate the frog for the Croydon direction. On 7th May 1954 the breakdown truck is in its usual place; 68 is the only B1 that can be identified. *London Transport Museum U5320*

The depot is seen before there is any indication of it being converted for buses. Three B1s, which had been there since inception day, are at the front of the building. 75, on the left, is having its nearside wheels attended to, while 76 is on the forecourt. 65, in the right-hand bay, shows PRIVATE and is the Carshalton trainer. The RTs are from nearby Sutton garage – they were parked here during off-peak times to alleviate space difficulties there. Trolleybus 65 and RT 277 (on the left) were both overhauled in July 1955 so ties this photo to being taken that month.
Don Thompson

On Sunday 2nd June 1957 the Southern Counties Touring Society hired the highest numbered trolleybus in the fleet. They embarked on a tour that saw them travelling as far north as Woodford and as far south as Carshalton and maybe even Sutton Green. Carshalton staff are amazed at Q1 1891 rubbing shoulders with the oldest trolleybuses in the fleet.
John L.Smith

Carshalton trolleybus depot has ceased trading so the **CARSHALTON GARAGE** title is entirely appropriate. 86, devoid of its valance, is being driven to Colindale scrapyard for breaking; it is 4th March 1959 and one of the first to leave. The driver takes the facing frog with power on and causes arcing; he doesn't care as the equipment is to all intents and purposes finished. On traction standard 472 a 'Buses for Trolleybuses' poster is seen; also on the pole is another oval white marker. The frog handle is not adjacent to it but it may have been re-positioned over the years. Two bikes are seen propped against the depot kerbstones; one belongs to the photographer. Carshalton was the only depot converted to trolleybuses pre-1939 that (apart from E2 622 at West Ham) retained any of its original vehicles right up to the time they were replaced by motorbuses during the trolleybus conversion programme.
John L.Smith

THE PALACE TO THE GREEN

Apart from its first two months when it operated between Sutton and West Croydon, route 654 worked between Crystal Palace and Sutton Green (the 654 route was known by crews as "The Palace to the Green"). In 1936, ten more short wheelbased vehicles were delivered; five (489 - 493) were fitted with coasting and runback brakes. They were initially used on miscellaneous work, with all eventually being allocated to Holloway depot; they found their way to Sutton/Carshalton, with 492 being the last one to arrive - in November 1952. 490, photographed at the Sutton terminus, met a premature end for when it went in for overhaul in July 1957 it was found to be in too bad a condition to make expenditure on it worthwhile. The fluted traction pole, which holds a flag with a description of the route, is inside private property; although not apparent the pole is painted silver, an early design experiment. Sutton Green was the most southerly trolleybus terminus on the London trolleybus system. Although 489 to 493 were officially classified as B1, they could be seen with a B3 inscription on the platform wall. *Alan Cross*

Due to some B1s being driven through heavy floodwater, Carshalton borrowed three J3s from Highgate depot in September 1958, spending nine days there. 1049 is CN 1 on route 654 and stands at the top of Anerley Hill, Crystal Palace. This was the first time that Carshalton drivers had to change a destination blind; SUTTON BUSHEY RD is displayed - until now they had been used to short wheel-based vehicles. The J3s were thirty foot long and were driven voluntarily – no doubt a few kerbs were clipped! The driver will have to put the coasting brake lever in to operation before he moves off. The only other vehicles that could have been used in this situation were Highgate's L1s.

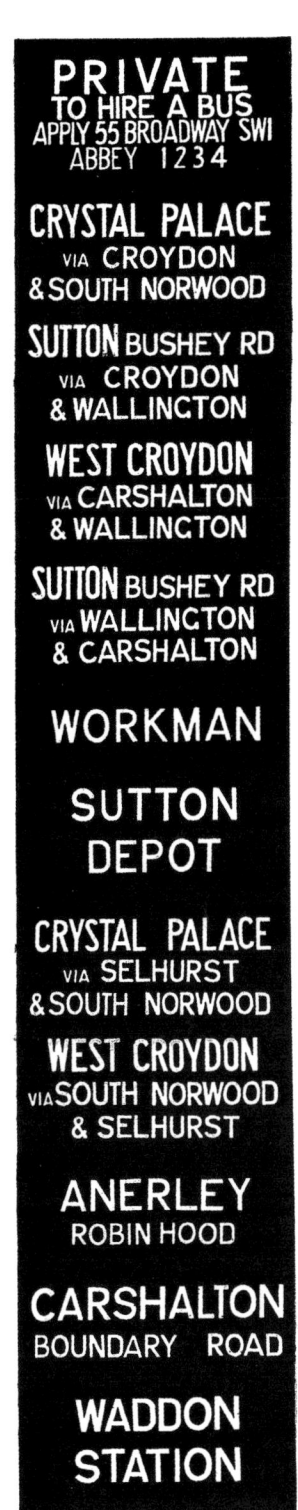

8.9.47

PRIVATE
TO HIRE A BUS OR COACH
APPLY: 55 BROADWAY S.W.1
ABBEY 1234

CRYSTAL PALACE
CROYDON
SOUTH NORWOOD

SUTTON BUSHEY RD
CROYDON
WALLINGTON

WEST CROYDON
VIA WALLINGTON

CARSHALTON
DEPOT

ANERLEY
VIA ROBIN HOOD

CARSHALTON
BOUNDARY ROAD

WADDON
STATION

8.3.56

EXTRA 654

18.3.49

EXTRA 654

30.10.57

PRIVATE
TO HIRE A BUS
APPLY
55 BROADWAY SW1
ABBEY 1234

SOUTH NORWOOD
SELHURST
WEST CROYDON
WALLINGTON

654

CROYDON
WADDON
WALLINGTON
BOUNDARY RD

13.2.51

PRIVATE
TO HIRE A BUS
APPLY. 55 BROADWAY S.W.1.
ABBEY. 1234

SOUTH NORWOOD
SELHURST
WEST CROYDON
WALLINGTON

654

CROYDON
WADDON
WALLINGTON
BOUNDARY RD

12.12.52

NOTES
The lower WEST CROYDON panel is inapplicable as there was no wiring facility to turn there from Crystal Palace. The ANERLEY panel should be VIA ROBIN HOOD - the implication is that the turn was at the Robin Hood pub which it wasn't.

No blinds were produced to show route 630. When operating on this service, Hammersmith destination blinds were used. Route blinds were turned to EXTRA and side blinds to a blank panel.

STAFF TROLLEYBUS JOURNEYS

CARSHALTON ROUTE 654

	Nights of Sun/Mon to Fri/Sat.			Night of Sat/Sun.			
	654	654	654	654	654		
Sutton (Bushey Road)	12.35			12.35			
Carshalton Depot	12.40	3. 2	5. 5	12.40	5.58		
Woodcote Road	12.50	3.12	5.15	12.50	6. 8		
West Croydon	1. 3	3.25	5.28	1. 3	6.21		
Anerley (Robin Hood)	1.18	3.40		1.18	6.36		
Crystal Palace	1.25	3.47		1.25	6.43		
Crystal Palace	1.27	3.50		1.27	6.46		
Anerley (Robin Hood)	1.34	3.57		1.34	6.53		
West Croydon	1.49	4.12	5.31	1.49	7. 8		
Woodcote Road	2. 2	4.25	5.44	2. 2	7.21		
Carshalton Depot	2.12	4.35	5.54	2.12	7.31		
Sutton (Bushey Road)			5.59		7.36		

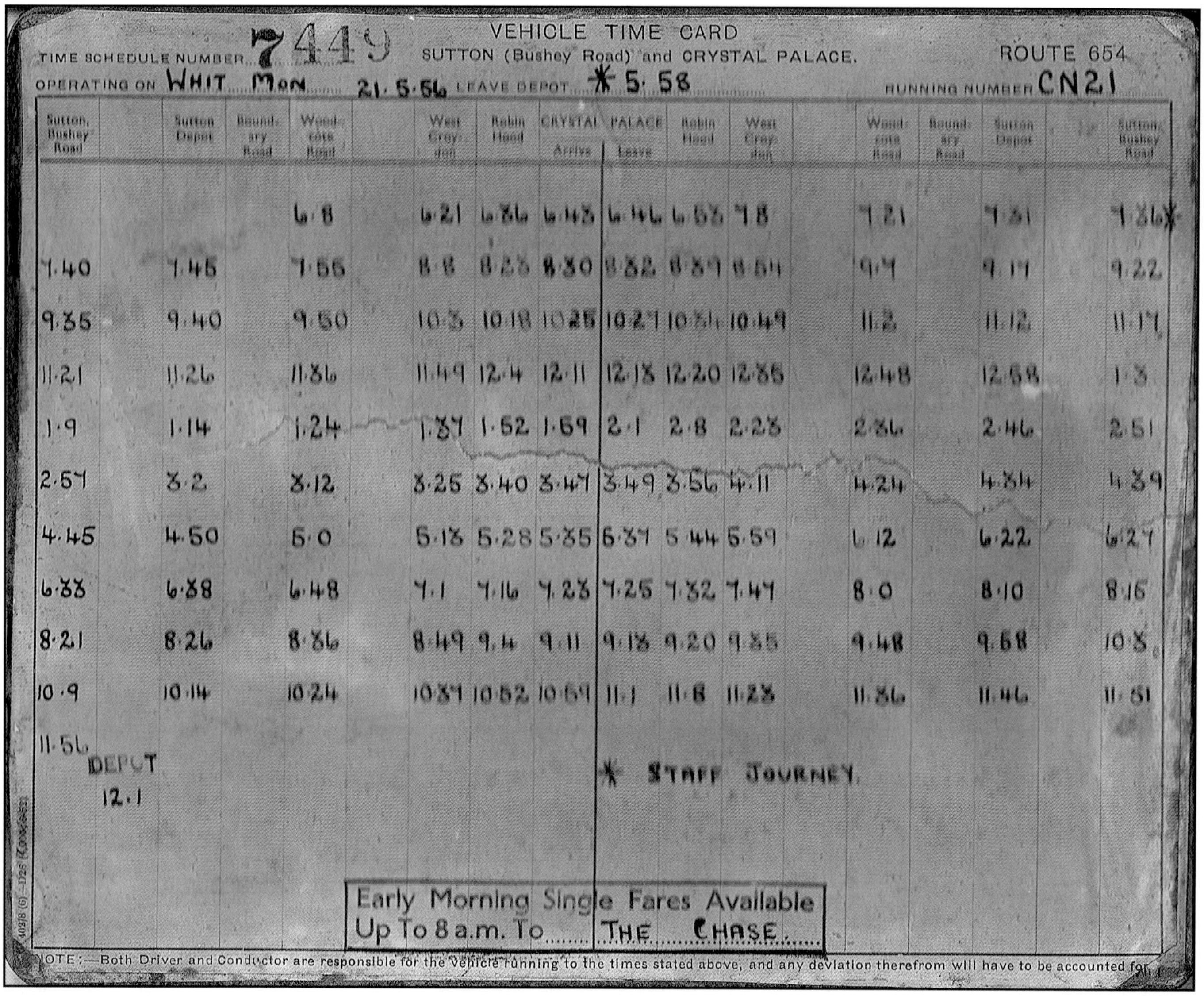

WANDSWORTH

Opened 12th September 1937. Four roads were for trolleybuses, the rest for trams. A trolleybus turntable-traverser was used though in a fixed position latterly. There were no proper docking pits; two permitted routine maintenance with vehicles receiving full attention at Hammersmith who loaned vehicles when shortfalls occurred; 433 and 553 are two examples. Intriguingly 520, which was allocated to Hammersmith when new on 12th September 1937, spent a month at Wandsworth between 21st October and 11th November that year before being returned to Hammersmith; it will never be known if 520 was deliberately chosen as it was the one above Wandsworth's permanent residents of 502 to 519. An interesting transfer here was 438 from Bexleyheath in November 1945 before onward movement to Hammersmith. The lack of facilities at Wandsworth saw vehicles deteriorate. It was the only depot to retain tram operation during its full lifetime as a trolleybus operator (September 1937 – September 1950). As at Holloway, staff were allocated to trams or trolleybuses, though there were a number who could crew both when required. Until 1944 the output of fourteen was the lowest in the fleet. When Wandsworth took on some 630s in April 1944 they were given D2s, 468, 474 and 475; they now had twenty-one vehicles for seventeen runnings. Bearing in mind the bad condition of Wandsworth's trolleybuses this could well be seen as appropriate.

Closed to trolleybuses on 30th September 1950.
Routes operated: 612, 628 (bank holidays), 630.
Type used: Leyland.
Capacity: 24 though the maximum requirement was 20. If the South London tram to trolleybus conversion had occurred it was anticipated that 86 trolleybuses could be housed.
Last trolleybus into depot: not known.

Wandsworth depot was situated in Carl Street; access to the' main line' in York Road was via Jews Row. Higgs and Hill are converting the depot for buses in August 1949. Trams use conduit for electrical pick-up; its use in the depot and immediately outside will soon be terminated. Overhead and traction poles will be erected and used until conversion day – the night of 30th September 1950. Although the track layout implies that cars use both exits that is not so – the one in view is only for trolleybuses, a situation pertaining since September 1937.
London Transport Museum U17058

It is September 1949. By now a change pit has been installed just inside the depot and trams use overhead inside. A number of cars, with trolleys on the wire, are parked on the left. Four D3 trolleybuses are in view with 518 and 506 having operated on route 612. Trams and trolleybuses all show WANDSWORTH STATION; this was incorrect as the nearby station was Wandsworth Town. The vehicle on the right has been out on the 630; part of NR WILLESDEN JUNCTION is revealed. The fact that EXTRA is used and that this is seen in another photograph of a Wandsworth 630 gives rise to the concept that these workings always showed EXTRA. They only ran in Monday to Saturday peaks and may hark back to tram days when Wandsworth put cars out with EX route plates when working extras on their tram services. The front advert on the unidentified 630 implies that the Government are trying to encourage people to save water during a drought. Tram 1773 is a 1922 series E1; by this time only two unmodified E1s survived in service at this depot – 1764 and 1773.

London Transport Museum U 15793

Wandsworth depot in the post-war era; of the four trams in view only E3 196 on road ten can be identified. The two dilapidated cars are former West Ham open-fronted cars here for storage; remnants of white paint are on their fenders, indicative of use on Barking Road tram services between September 1939 and June 1940. These were two of a number of cars taken to Hampstead depot for storage in case they were needed as replacement cars during wartime. This was not necessary but a fire at the depot in 1946 saw all trams being removed and sent to various locations. These cars never ran again and were broken up in due course. On the extreme right a D3 has run in off route 612.

E3 car 1954 leaves the depot for BORO & LONDON BGE on route 12; adjacent to it is tower wagon 728J (formerly STL 401). Trolleybus wires are seen above this adapted vehicle. *Fred Ivey*

D3 506 is on the 612 Battersea terminal stand during the last month of the route – September 1950. Wandsworth was first to have a combined depot and running number holder; however, these were not used and 506 suffices with the old style running number wedged in place. The conductor has wound the blind round a bit too far so part of the previous display is shown. BUSH GREEN is the bottom part of SHEPHERDS BUSH GREEN, a short working on route 630. *Alan Cross*

> Wandsworth Tram Depot. Turntable Traverser to be removed and refitted at Edmonton Trolleybus Depot. W.E's est. £545.
> With the replacement of trams by motor buses at this Depot, the traverser will become redundant, and it is proposed that it be dismantled and re-assembled at Edmonton where one only is at present available, which gives rise to considerable congestion and delay during the run-in.
>
> It was confirmed that provision had already been made in the S.E.R. covering the major project at Wandsworth for the dismantling of this traverser; therefore the only costs chargeable to this transfer were charges arising from the conveyance of the traverser from Wandsworth to Edmonton and its installation at the latter depot.   The C.M.E.
>
> DIRECTED: that Mr.Schofield advise the split of the cost of £545 between the two separate jobs.

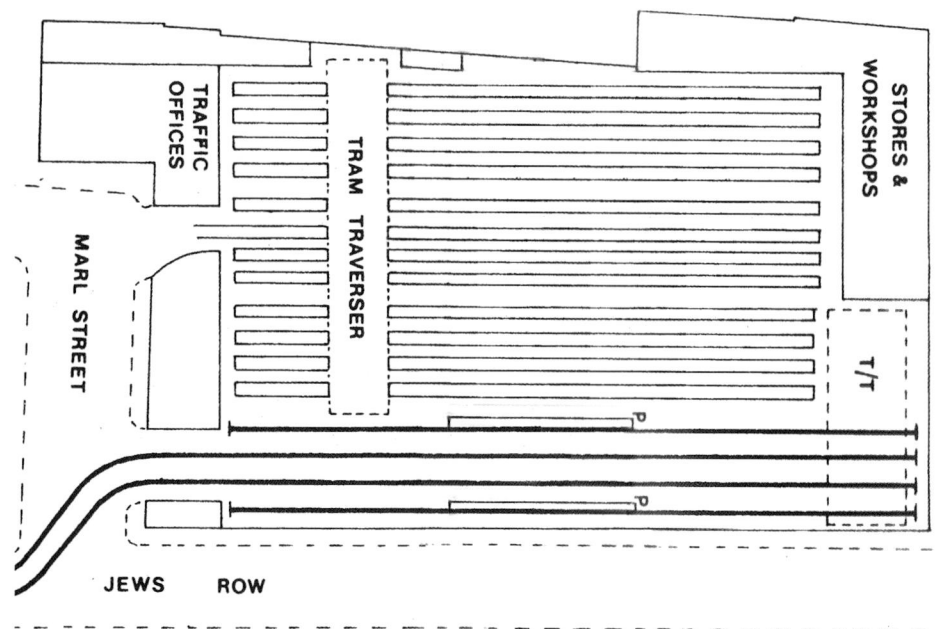

Traffic circular items for 1938.

1853.—ROUTE No. 628—WHIT-MONDAY.

Notice to Inspectors and Conductors—Wandsworth Depot.

On Whit-Monday certain Route No. 628 trolleybuses will operate from Wandsworth Depot.
A farebill is exhibited in the depot and must be closely studied.
When running to and from Wandsworth Depot fares will be charged and tickets punched as for St. John's Hospital.
Destination Blinds must be set as follows :—

When Running.	Front and Rear.	Side Blind.
Clapham Junction	8 { Clapham Junction via Harlesden	{ Wandsworth Putney 3 { Hammersmith Shepherds Bush Harlesden
Scrubs Lane	12 { Nr. Willesden Junction via Putney	
Wandsworth Depot	2 { Wandsworth Depot	—

1855.—ROUTE No. 628 TO OPERATE ON WHIT-MONDAY.

Notice to Inspectors and Conductors—Hanwell Depot.

On Whit-Monday certain Route No. 628 trolleybuses will operate from Hanwell Depot. A farebill is exhibited in the depot and must be carefully studied.

Tickets.

Route No. 655 tickets will be supplied for use when running between Hanwell Depot and Hammersmith Broadway and Route No. 628 tickets for use during the service journeys.

Destination Blinds.

Special blinds containing the required wording will be used and the following destinations must be shown :—

When Running to	Front and Rear.	Side Blind.
Clapham Junction	8 { Clapham Junction via Harlesden	{ Wandsworth Putney 3 { Hammersmith Shepherds Bush Harlesden
Scrubs Lane	12 { Nr. Willesden Junction via Putney	
Hammersmith	3 { Hammersmith Broadway	
Hanwell Depot	1 { Private	

PRIVATE
WANDSWORTH STATION
HAMMERSMITH BROADWAY
TOOTING
CRAVEN PARK
SHEPHERDS BUSH GREEN
MITCHAM FAIR GREEN VIA TOOTING
BATTERSEA PRINCES HEAD
WORKMAN
CLAPHAM JUNCTION VIA HARLESDEN
ACTON MARKET PLACE
ACTON
CRAVEN PARK VIA HARLESDEN & HAMMERSMITH
NTH ACTON STN
NR WILLESDEN JUNCTION VIA PUTNEY & TOOTING
WEST CROYDON
SUMMERSTOWN

24.1.50

Operation of Route 630 from Wandsworth Depot 3403

Wandsworth Depot

Commencing on Wednesday, 19th April, 1944, certain Trolleybuses on Route 630 will operate from Wandsworth Depot. For the purpose of duty schedules Route 630 duties will be combined with those of Route 612.

Specimens of the revised tickets are exhibited in the depot.

A Route 630 farebill will also be shown.

Attention is called to the 3d. workman return fares issued between West Croydon and Tooting Station and to the consequential 5d., 7d. and 9d. through workman fares.

DESTINATION BLINDS

The following wordings must be shown :—

When Running to	Show			
	Front and Rear		Side	
Harrow Road	No. 12	{ Nr. Willesden Junction via Putney	No. 4	{ Croydon Mitcham Tooting Putney Hammersmith
West Croydon	13	{ via Putney and Tooting W. Croydon		
Wandsw'th Depot	2	Wandsworth Station		—

HAMMERSMITH

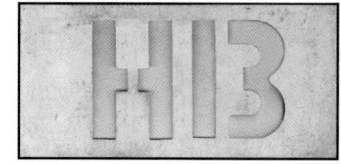

Opened 12th September 1937. The building fronted onto Great Church Lane; there was access at the rear via Hammersmith Road but only for ancillary vehicles. In conjunction with an adjacent new road, Butterwick, in 1958 a corner of the building was removed. *HB stands for Hammersmith Broadway.*

Closed to trolleybuses on 19th July 1960.
Routes operated: 626, 628, 630, 660, 666.
Type used: Leyland.
Capacity under cover was 65.
Number of vehicles licensed in March 1951 was 75.
Last trolleybus into depot under its own power: 1121 - route 630.
N.B. 1161 on route 630 was the last HB trolleybus in service but had to be towed into the depot as the traction current had been switched off before it got there.

This view shows the unique arrangement that existed at Hammersmith tram depot - a traverser fitted externally rather than internally. In October 1936 a London Transport Guy back-up vehicle appears to be towing a tram out of the building; a petrol pump of some sort for motor vehicles is in front of the central traction pole. The dual overhead wires imply trolleybus type construction; this is not so as they are purely entry and exit wires. A number of E1 trams have run in off route 30; the depot had a schedule requirement of about forty so was considerably enlarged to accommodate a trolleybus requirement of around seventy.
London Transport Museum H16089

The two views on this page were taken on 7th May 1939 with vehicles blinded for the three main routes operated here - 626/628/630. At the front of the four lines of trolleybuses are D3 543, D2s 432, 462 and D3 529. The D2s are second-hand from Hanwell, the D3s new to Hammersmith. Only 543 shows the correct blind display; the others are misnomers so maybe the photographer wanted different panels displayed. 529 and 543 retain their chrome windscreens. Those on the D2s have been painted red on overhaul as part of the Board's latest policy; they were also given red front domes at the same time. The D3s have not yet been overhauled. In the background a couple of trolleybuses are parked over the pits. Troughing dances around the depot.

London Transport Museum U29695

Most trolleybuses in this view are D2s/D3s. It is a Sunday and vehicle movements are few so the photographer has arranged for the vehicles to be especially positioned for the view. The most interesting vehicle in this picture is K2 1322 which was delivered on 7th February and licensed two days later; maybe it is covering for D class vehicles undergoing their first overhaul. In the late 1930's there were many instances of brand new trolleybuses helping out to keep depots' allocations topped up. Even not-so-new machines would cover for short-term needs with H1s 766/767 here on 9th July 1938. As in the previous view, the vehicles have been especially positioned for the London Transport photographer. 1322 moved to Hackney in time for trolleybus conversion on 10th June 1939.

London Transport Museum U29697.

On 7th May 1939 D3 544 is next to tower wagon 85Q. There are two lines of overhead for both entry and exit; later in the year one entry wire was removed. The office on the left of the building is in the same style as Bexleyheath. Above the entrance HAMMERSMITH TROLLEY BUS DEPOT is declared; the words TROLLEY and BUS have not been joined as they should have been. The same occurred at Ilford.

London Transport Museum U29699

On 7th November 1943, D3 530 suffered blast damage near Putney Bridge. This photograph was taken in Hammersmith depot the day after and shows the effectiveness of mesh stuck across windows - mesh protected passengers from flying glass and injury. Four employees each hold a window. Staff have decided to take the blinds out of the vehicle.

London Transport Museum U53260

In the late evening of Sunday 20th February 1944 C2 184 was the victim of an air raid in Glenthorne Road, Hammersmith; all the windows were broken, there was shrapnel damage to the offside and nearside and upper deck blast damage. 184, the first C2, belonged to Stonebridge but the recovery crew towed it to nearby Hammersmith depot where it was photographed the next day. It cost £200 to repair which in today's money is about £8350. *London Transport Museum U35433*

The reader will notice that there is an imbalance of photographs between depots. The newly formed London Transport used freelance photographers who had top class equipment to record important aspects of its operations which included new trolleybus depots. A large number of views were taken at Hounslow, Bexleyheath and Sutton with many being used in the Transport Press to show other operators the latest design and how London Transport was at the forefront of efficient stabling. After that, photography was greatly scaled down and at Finchley, Hendon, Stonebridge and Hanwell there are few images. As more depots were commissioned London Transport seemed to lose interest and apart from the final tram to trolleybus change-over at Poplar those in the north and east of the system were not photographed on inception. Some war damage was recorded and all were dealt with in one fell swoop in May 1954 by freelancer Colin Tait.

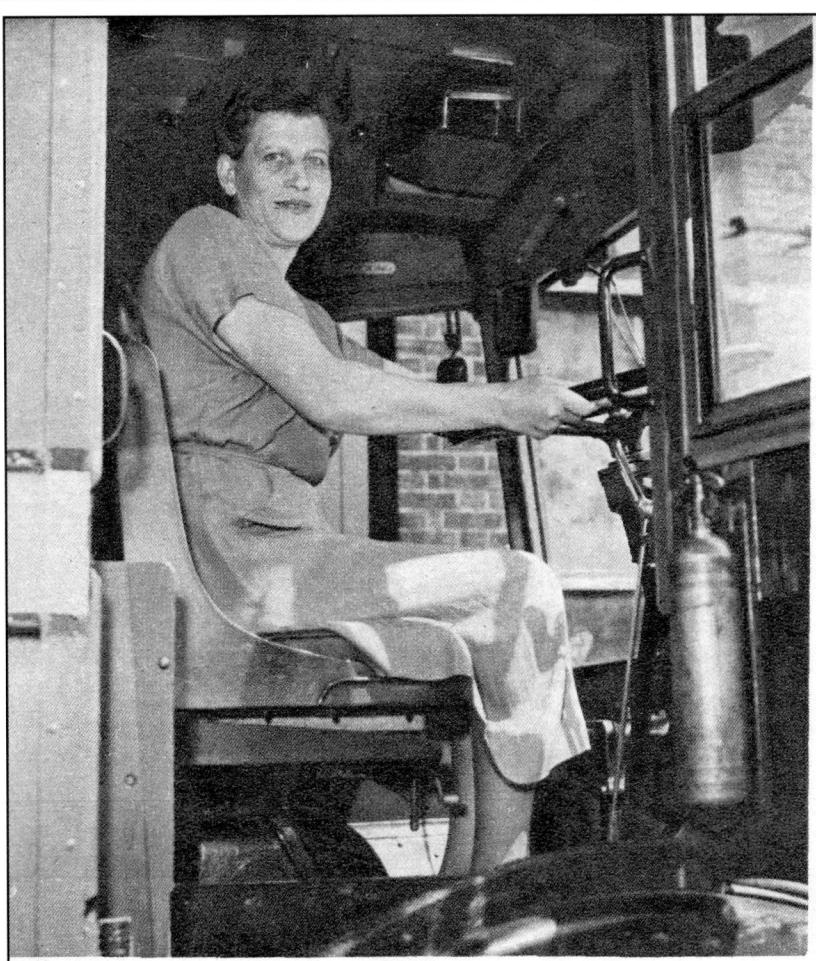

VISITORS FROM MOSCOW

Left: *Mrs. P. A. Fedina, who is a trolleybus driver in Moscow and was the only woman member of the party, at the wheel of one of our trolleybuses at Hammersmith depot.*

Extract from July 1956 London Transport Magazine.

Staff visits from abroad occurred in post-war years. In 1956, Mrs P.A. Fedina, a Moscow trolleybus driver (single deckers only) inspects the cab of one of Hammersmith's vehicles in the depot. There were a number of London Transport officials in attendance - no doubt there were many volunteers to help her get in the cab! What wouldn't she have given to take it out for a spin on the 630.

The original façade of Hammersmith depot is seen in 1954 with two P1s in view; there is only one set of wires for entry now. The building fronts onto Great Church Lane. The lettering above the entrance states LONDON TRANSPORT HAMMERSMITH TROLLEYBUS DEPOT. Compare this view to that on page 230 and it will be seen that 'TROLLEYBUS' is now spelt correctly. On the left, wooden gates lead to other parts of the premises.
London Transport Museum U5353.

On loan from Lea Bridge depot one day in the early 1950's. K2 1327 has been out on the 628. It was a long trek to get here but it was vital that fleet strengths were maintained; maybe it was the nearest depot with a spare vehicle. Ironically, 1327 returned to Hammersmith on a permanent basis in April 1959 in connection with stage two of the trolleybus conversion scheme. Alongside, D3 507 shows 630 CLAPHAM JUNCTION; a few journeys on this route were scheduled to run off-line of route - bifurcating at Wandsworth.
Don Jones

Opening in July 1958 a one-way system at Hammersmith led to repercussions for trolleybuses entering and leaving the depot; the widening of Great Church Lane saw temporary wiring layouts for a while. D3 510 departs as a 628 to Harlesden. Trolleybuses cannot pass each other here so drivers need to keep a sharp look-out to avoid getting themselves into difficulties. Great Church Lane is still a two-way road. *Fred Ivey*

There was little room between the back of the depot and the maintenance area; therefore it was difficult to get pictures of trolleybuses in this part of the building. The photographer has leant back as far as he can to capture P1 1706, K1 1069 and others over the pits. The second and fourth vehicles show HAMMERSMITH BROADWAY/ HAMMERSMITH DEPOT - 1069 shows DEPOT HAMMERSMITH. A driver has saved himself a couple of twirls on the destination blind handle. *Tony Belton*

Sent to Hammersmith depot in May 1960 was H1 780 which has been driven the length of the depot on battery power. Far easier for staff to come off the traverser and not put booms on the wires; a bamboo pole rests sloppily against 780 - the next driver will have to move it up a few feet to get the poles on the wires. 780 has correctly been positioned - in front of a NO PARKING sign on the depot floor. Breakdown tender 737J awaits a call-out.
Fred Ivey

It was standard practice for shunting staff, having left the traverser, to use battery power to park up; long-time resident 524 and a number of other trolleybuses illustrate this. 747 has been involved in some sort of prang – it has been towed in and awaits the coachmakers' attention.
John L. Smith

The 1958 one-way system at Hammersmith saw external alterations made to the depot; the office wall was heavily modified and gained a curved side with extra windows; new brickwork shows up against the old. The side of the building had been out of view but is now open to public gaze and smartened up. LONDON TRANSPORT HAMMERSMITH TROLLEYBUS DEPOT is seen on the side of the premises – this was the only instance of a depot having two signs. 1279 turns out of Butterwick on route 628; RTL 1547 on route 11 follows. Note the A219 road sign on a traffic bollard.
Tony Belton

By the time this view was taken shortly before the depot closed it could be very difficult to leave. This is well illustrated by F1 743 departing for BROADWAY TOOTING on route 630; metaphorically speaking the driver 'fights his way out of the building'.
Don Lewis

The interior is seen on its final day of operation, 19th July 1960. Trolleybus tools hang on a wall; outside the store are a number of trolleybus accoutrements. The turntable/traverser will not be used much longer. To the left, a doorway leads into Hammersmith Road.
John Gillham

FOUR CLASSES OF LEYLANDS

TRUE-FORM AND F.W.WOOLWORTH have long disappeared from the retail scene. They were still trading in Wandsworth High Street when 456 paused on its way to NR WILLESDEN JUNCTION on route 630; this terminology was copied from the tram era. It was not until the mid-fifties that it was re-named HARLESDEN COLLEGE PARK – a public house at the top of Scrubs Lane, not a recreational facility.

F1s started to drift into Hammersmith depot in mid-1958; arriving in January 1959 was 746 which stayed until the depot closed. Advertising Danish bacon and butter, 746 is first away from the traffic lights at the junction of Fulham High Street with New Kings Road on 20th April 1959; a pack of motor vehicles follow as it heads for Clapham Junction on route 628.

John Clarke

Although London's trolleybuses were just about the largest vehicles on the road by the time 1960 came round the volume of traffic in the capital saw them juggling for road space as much as any vehicle; this is apparent in this view of K2 1162 turning into Fulham Palace Road. The rear of an RFW Private Hire coach can be seen; in the background is Hammersmith depot from where 1162 has just left as a 626 to Clapham Junction. *Tony Belton*

P1 1703 left Craven Park Circle a few minutes before this view was taken in Craven Park Road on 13th March 1955. The linen number blind sits comfortably with the 'paper' produced one. Hot drink advertisements are not a new concept – Lyons is marketing BEV coffee and consider it worthwhile to advertise between Harlesden and Clapham Junction on route 628. All of 1703's windows are closed on what must be a cold day.

Peter Mitchell 6823

Blind 1 (6.2.50)

PRIVATE

FULHAM PALACE RD
(EDGARLEY TERRACE)

HAMMERSMITH
BROADWAY
TOOTING
CRAVEN
PARK
SHEPHERDS
BUSH GREEN

MITCHAM
FAIR GREEN
VIA TOOTING
BATTERSEA
PRINCES HEAD

WORKMAN

CLAPHAM
JUNCTION
VIA HARLESDEN
ACTON
MARKET PLACE
ACTON

CRAVEN PARK
VIA HARLESDEN
& HAMMERSMITH
NTH ACTON STN

NR WILLESDEN
JUNCTION
VIA PUTNEY
& TOOTING
WEST CROYDON

SUMMERSTOWN

6.2.50

Blind 2 (16.8.56)

PRIVATE
TO HIRE A BUS OR COACH
APPLY: 55 BROADWAY S.W.1
ABBEY 1234

FULHAM PALACE RD
EDGARLEY TERRACE

HAMMERSMITH
DEPOT
HAMMERSMITH
BROADWAY
TOOTING
HARLESDEN
CRAVEN PARK
SHEPHERDS
BUSH GREEN

MITCHAM
(FAIR GREEN)
VIA TOOTING
CLAPHAM
JUNCTION
VIA HARLESDEN
ACTON
(MARKET PLACE)
HARLESDEN
CRAVEN PARK
VIA HAMMERSMITH
NTH. ACTON STN

HARLESDEN
(COLLEGE PARK)
VIA PUTNEY
TOOTING
WEST CROYDON

SUMMERSTOWN

16.8.56

Blind 3 (4.3.60)

PRIVATE
TO HIRE A BUS OR COACH
APPLY: 55 BROADWAY S.W.1
ABBEY 5600

FULHAM PALACE RD
EDGARLEY TERRACE

HAMMERSMITH
DEPOT
HAMMERSMITH
BROADWAY
TOOTING
HARLESDEN
CRAVEN PARK
SHEPHERDS BUSH
GREEN

MITCHAM
FAIR GREEN
VIA TOOTING
CLAPHAM
JUNCTION
VIA HARLESDEN
ACTON
MARKET PLACE
HARLESDEN
CRAVEN PARK
VIA HAMMERSMITH
NTH. ACTON STN

HARLESDEN
COLLEGE PARK
VIA PUTNEY
TOOTING
WEST CROYDON

SUMMERSTOWN

4.3.60

Blind 4 (8.3.55)

EXTRA
628
626
630
660

8.3.55

Blind 5 (26.6.51)

PRIVATE
TO HIRE A BUS
APPLY
55 BROADWAY SW1
ABBEY 1234

612
WANDSWORTH
EARLSFIELD
TOOTING
MITCHAM

612

628
WANDSWORTH
PUTNEY
HAMMERSMITH
HARLESDEN
ACTON

626
MITCHAM
TOOTING
WANDSWORTH
HAMMERSMITH

630
TOOTING
WANDSWORTH
PUTNEY
HAMMERSMITH

628

660
JUBILEE CLOCK
OLD OAK LANE
NTH ACTON STN
ACTON

26.6.51

NOTES

The 6.2.50 blind should be compared with the Wandsworth blind on page 227; the Wandsworth display has been removed and FULHAM PALACE ROAD inserted.

The introduction of paper blinds saw an anomoly eradicated. Until now there had been confusion to passengers on northbound 626/628/630s running into Hammersmith depot - this was due to the fact that they were not going as far as Hammersmith Broadway; they turned right into Great Church Lane to access the depot. To allay complaints HAMMERSMITH DEPOT was added so that passengers knew vehicles were not going as far as the Broadway.

The lack of brackets on the 4.3.60 blind should be compared with the 16.8.56 blind.

660 displays on side and route blinds are irrelevant as Hammersmith ceased operating before the blinds were made.

The 26.6.51 blind has details for route 612 which finished nine months earlier; intriguingly it incorporates a display for the day 612 and the night 612. Additionally, Hammersmith did not work route 612. The lower 628 display is for the night route which was withdrawn at the end of September 1950. The Boards and Blinds Department are not up to speed with the Traffic Department!

It is Tuesday 19th July 1960, conversion stage seven. K2 1176 has carried its last passengers and has run in off route 630. Somebody is about to remove its front blinds before it is transferred to Colindale depot for storage. Hammersmith depot is in its last hours of use; BEA coaches will operate from here the next day - a few have already arrived.

Tony Belton

STAFF TROLLEYBUS JOURNEYS

HAMMERSMITH Route 630

	Nights of Sun/Mon to Fri/Sat.				Night of Sat/Sun.			
	630	630	630	640	630	630	630	
West Croydon		1.48	2.57			1.48	4. 6	
Mitcham (Fair Green)		2. 8	3.17			2. 8	4.26	
Tooting Broadway		2.16	3.25			2.16	4.34	
Wandsworth High Street			3.40			2.31	4.49	
Wimbledon Stadium		2.20						
Putney Bridge Road						2.37		
Putney High Street			3.46				4.55	
Fulham Palace Road			3.55			2.46	5. 4	A To connect with Route 630 night bus arriving 2.29
Hammersmith Depot	12. 7			4.37	12. 7			
Shepherds Bush						2.54		B To connect with Route 662 first bus from Paddington.
Harrow Road	12.26		4.13	4.53 B	12.26		5.22	
Harrow Road	12.29		4.16	4.58	12.29		5.24	
Shepherds Bush						2.58		
Hammersmith Depot			4.33				5.44	
Fulham Palace Road	12.48			5.17	12.48	3. 6		**These connections were the only instance of a night trolleybus connecting with a staff trolleybus.**
Putney High Street								
Putney Bridge Road	12.59			5.26	12.57	3.15		
Wimbledon Stadium		2.25						
Wandsworth High Street	1. 3	A			1. 3	3.21		
Tooting Broadway	1.18	2.29			1.18	3.36		
Mitcham (Fair Green)	1.26	2.37			1.26	3.44		
West Croydon	1.46	2.55			1.46	4. 4		

CHISWICK TRAM DEPOT

This former London United Tramways depot acted as an overnight overspill to Hammersmith depot for a few weeks in 1937 until rebuilding was completed there. A single set of wires led from Chiswick High Road which was useful as 'light' overhauls commenced here in early 1938; this ceased in 1939 when Charlton was up to strength. The wires were removed (probably in wartime) but before the re-commencement of overhauling in the spring of 1946. Towing was the means of arrival but some may have made their own way there and used batteries to enter. Overhauling/renovation ceased for good in November 1951. As many as fourteen vehicles could be worked on simultaneously. New vehicles were stored here.

Routes operated: 626, 628, 630.
Type used: Leyland.
Capacity: Not known.

(Top and above) No views have materialised of trolleybuses being dealt with at Chiswick tram depot; however two vestiges of electric traction are captured on film. Looking into the premises from Chiswick High Road on 3rd December 1955 a single traction pole is seen; tram track also remains. Earlier, on 24th April 1951, the intrepid Mr Gillham photographed the building where trolleybuses are being dealt with - if only he had gone inside with his camera. Outside are a Q type coach blinded for route 715 and an STL. The traction standard on the left is a remnant of overhead wiring here.

John Gillham

445 was a notable vehicle in the trolleybus fleet as it retained its half cab with a seat positioned alongside the driver until the end of its days in April 1959. It is not known why it is at Chiswick Works on 10th September 1948 though there may be a clue in that it had been released from overhaul at Fulwell on 30th August. D2 445 belongs to Hammersmith who had 'joint blinds' with Wandsworth, hence the 612 display. The description of this photo is 'Showing pick-up' – it seems the breakdown tender is using a new type of towing bar which is being demonstrated. An STL bus on learner duties is in the background.
London Transport Museum U44702/44705

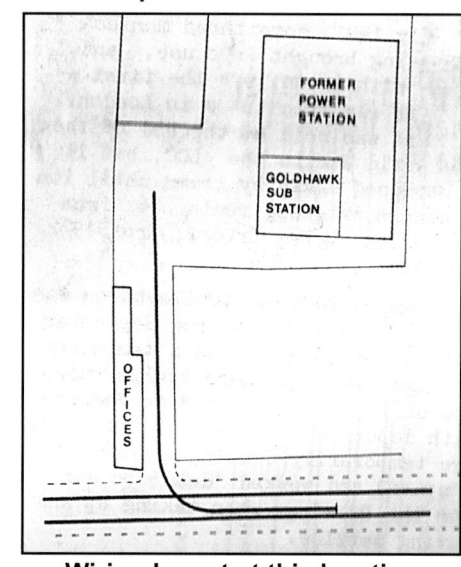

Wiring layout at this location

FULWELL

Opened 16th May 1931; operated trams and trolleybuses until 26th October 1935. Despite being in a relatively safe part of London it still suffered wartime problems. On 10th October 1940 one vehicle was damaged (trolleybus 40 was quoted as being on fire); on 19th February 1944 the depot was in darkness due to lighting arrangements being severed. Following the near destruction of Bexleyheath and West Ham depots in the summer of 1944 some vehicles were dispersed from various depots at night; this turned out to be counterproductive here as twelve stabled on the main road were damaged by enemy action on 22nd August 1944. There were two entrances/exits to the depot; Stanley Road and Wellington Road; it was also a 'run-through' depot. Fulwell was in the habit of putting anything that was available 'on the road' on busy days such as Bank Holidays. This included brand new vehicles and any that had just been overhauled but not returned to their depots.

Closed to trolleybuses on 8th May 1962.
Routes operated: 601, 601A, 602, 603, 604, 605, 667.
Type used: AEC and BUT.
Capacity under cover was 120.
Number of vehicles allocated in March 1951 was 92
Last trolleybus into depot: 1521 - route 604.

The Wellington Road entrance to the Fulwell depot of the London United Tramways Company is seen in June 1924; it was their largest and the hub of operations for trams in the Kingston and Twickenham areas. Prominent in the foreground is a scissors crossover. Either side of the tracks, flowerbeds are tidily kept; these were removed in trolleybus days to give better manoeuvrability. When the overhauling of trolleybuses commenced, the two sections of the building to the right of the picture were adapted for this purpose; the three arched windows near the far end were removed and replaced by sliding doors. *London Transport Museum U1586*

Parked in front of the ivy clad building are a number of 'Diddlers'; identifiable are 15, 37 and 16. Number 37 still carries a London United Tramways fleet-name which is missing on 15; this dates this view as taken shortly after the formation of the LPTB on 1st July 1933. Number 37 is on the loop that enables trolleybuses to move from the Wellington Road end of the depot to the Stanley Road end. In the top right-hand corner a tram overhead frog can be seen; trams are now kept in the southern part of the depot. *London Transport Museum U23457*

Seen in September 1934 maintenance staff work on an unidentified 'Diddler' without a fleet name; they use an air pressure gun to lubricate some of the working parts - access is via the detachable front panel. The vehicle is fitted with an LUT destination blind as is A1 28 on the left – A2 49 on the right uses a London Transport one. Until a new docking section was built in the mid-thirties this was the maintenance area; it later became Fulwell Works. The two trolleybuses nearest the camera have their positive boom on the single tram wire in the troughing; negative booms are on wires which have been strung alongside them. A bamboo pole hangs from the nearside boom of the unidentified trolleybus; another is hooked onto a rafter. By looking closely at the support for the overhead within the roof it is apparent that this is very much a makeshift and primitive affair.
London Transport Museum U15913

Photos and text about Fulwell Works will appear in a later volume.

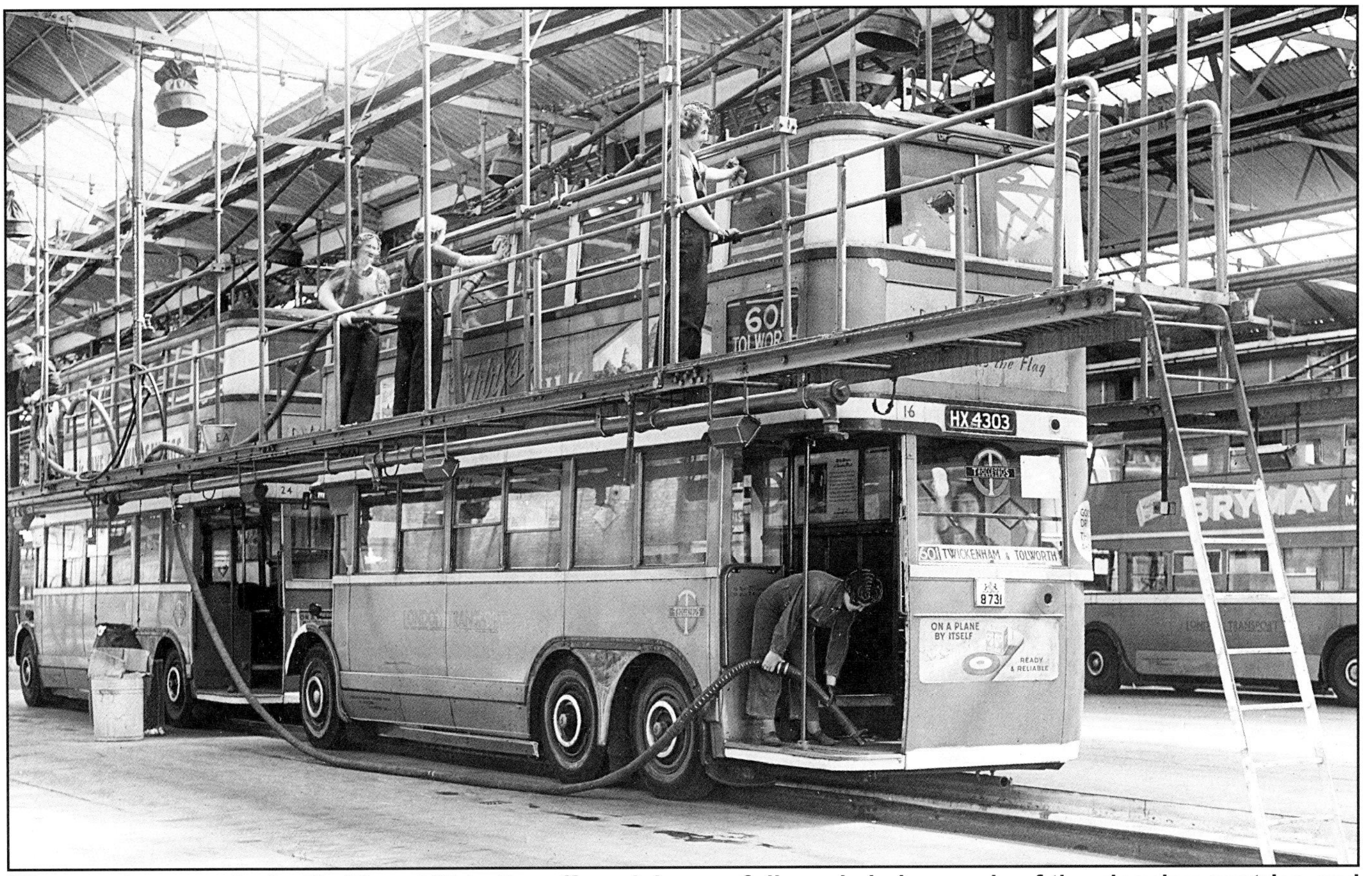

Women cleaners deal with 16 and 24 in the off-peak hours; full use is being made of the cleaning gantries and vacuum cleaners. The mesh on the vehicles' windows was a wartime measure as were the heavily shrouded lamps in the depot roof.

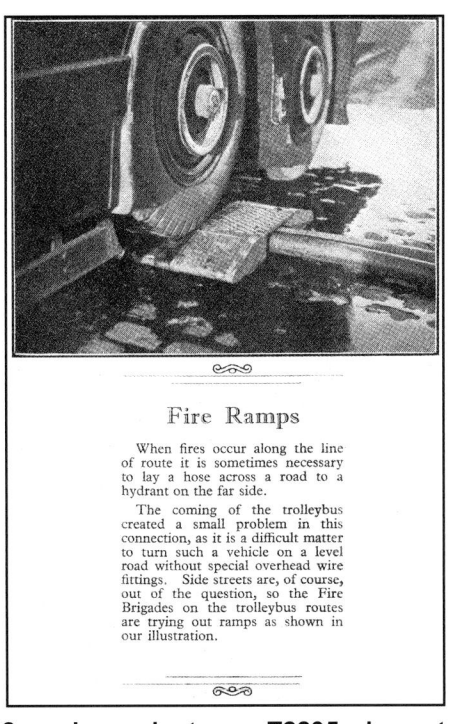

Fire Ramps

When fires occur along the line of route it is sometimes necessary to lay a hose across a road to a hydrant on the far side.

The coming of the trolleybus created a small problem in this connection, as it is a difficult matter to turn such a vehicle on a level road without special overhead wire fittings. Side streets are, of course, out of the question, so the Fire Brigades on the trolleybus routes are trying out ramps as shown in our illustration.

SA1 1722 and conductress T2295 do not go together! She cannot be nicknamed 'clippie' as a TIM ticket machine is at her waist. 'Clippie' was attributed to ladies using a Bell punch machine, the system used at Ilford depot where 1722, the first of the South-African vehicles diverted to London Transport, will spend its entire life. Fulwell conductors used TIM machines; this lady is posing for the photographer. This was one of a number of photographs especially taken in Fulwell depot to show these non-standard vehicles.

London Transport Museum U33505

Various trolleybuses were formally photographed at the Stanley Road end of the depot. Q1 1772, which judging by its appearance has just been released from the adjacent overhaul shops, has an 'LT DEPOT' configuration on its blind. Released from overhaul on 15th July 1958, and photographed the same day, is P1 1703 which is dressed as a Fulwell vehicle; it belongs to Hammersmith depot. The display for Tolworth 'Red Lion' does not incorporate the word VIA and the pub name is in brackets. Both vehicles have FW code plates.

London Transport Museum H6622/U21894

The photographer then turns to the rear of 1703; note that the route number is of the 'paper' variety while the front route blind (seen on the previous page) is linen. The hand painted finish of the vehicle is top class and the vehicle gleams in the sunlight. One of the last jobs to be carried out on 1703 was the fitting of advertisements.

London Transport Museum U21891

Bamboo Trolley Poles　　2870

The import of bamboo trolley poles owing to war conditions has ceased and those which are now in stock cannot be replaced. Drivers and Conductors are asked to exercise the greatest possible care to avoid damage and breakage.

Replacing of Bamboo Trolley Poles　　3108

The attention of trolleybus conductors is drawn to the danger to pedestrians and staff when passing behind trolleybuses through bamboo trolley poles projecting beyond the end of the Container. Care should be taken to avoid this.

Bamboo Poles　　68

Additional supplies of bamboo poles have now been obtained in order that each trolleybus may be supplied with one as part of the standard equipment.

The co-operation of all staff is sought to ensure that these poles are not damaged through insufficient care in handling them or lost through failure to replace them in the receptacle provided underneath each trolleybus.

Staff should not allow the poles to fall to the ground as this causes the bamboo to split.

Two 'Diddlers' (one being 24) have carried their last passengers; a trip to a breakers yard will soon occur. These ancient vehicles were replaced in 1948 by Q1s such as 1773. As detailed on the next page, number 24 spent a short time at Hammersmith as a tuition vehicle. 1773 was taken into stock on 12th May 1948 and licensed for service on 20th May. This meant that both vehicles were operational simultaneously. *Don Jones*

Good use was made of the ailing Diddlers; thirty-one were used as learners though some only operated in this capacity for about a month. Three (5, 11 and 20) worked only at Fulwell; twenty-eight spread their wings; Holloway and West Ham each operated three simultaneously. Many were abruptly delicensed on 1st June 1949.

Vehicle No	Depot	Date of Allocation	Date of withdrawal*
5	Fulwell	1st November 1948	1st June 1949
6	Finchley	24th November 1948	1st June 1949
7	Hammersmith	7th September 1948	18th May 1950
11	Fulwell	1st November 1948	1st January 1951
13	Edmonton	11th November 1948	1st January 1951
14	Hanwell	27th May 1948	1st August 1948
15	Hanwell	9th November 1948	1st June 1949
17	Holloway	24th November 1948	1st June 1949
19	Holloway	24th November 1948	1st January 1951
20	Fulwell	1st July 1948	3rd September 1948
24	Hammersmith	1st August 1948	3rd September 1948
28	West Ham	21st December 1948	1st June 1949
29	Hanwell	1st August 1948	9th November 1948
32	Stamford Hill	1st December 1948	1st January 1951
33	Holloway	1st December 1948	1st January 1951
36	Bow	1st August 1948	3rd September 1948
37	Finchley	9th November 1948	1st January 1951
39	Edmonton	1st August 1948	1st December 1948
40	Finchley	1st August 1948	9th November 1948
41	West Ham	1st December 1948	1st June 1949
42	Holloway	1st August 1948	24th November 1948
43	Holloway	1st August 1948	24th November 1948
45	Stamford Hill	1st August 1948	1st December 1948
46	Walthamstow	21st December 1948	1st June 1949
48	Stonebridge	9th November 1948	1st January 1951
52	Bow	7th September 1948	1st June 1949
53	Stonebridge	1st August 1948	9th November 1948
54	Walthamstow	7th September 1948	1st January 1951
57	Walthamstow	1st August 1948	3rd September 1948
58	West Ham	21st December 1948	1st November 1950
59	West Ham	1st August 1948	1st December 1948

* First day of delicensing.

This table illustrates 'Diddlers' licensed as Fulwell trainers; all went on to be full-time tuition vehicles at other locations.

6	1st November 1948 to 23rd November 1948
7	1st September 1948 to 6th September 1948
13	1st November 1948 to 10th November 1948
14	1st May 1948 to 26th May 1948
15	1st November 1948 to 8th November 1948
17	1st November 1948 to 23rd November 1948
19	1st November 1948 to 23rd November 1948
24	1st June 1948 to 31st July 1948
28	10th December 1948 to 20th December 1948
29	1st May 1948 to 31st July 1948
37	1st November 1948 to 8th November 1948
41	1st September 1948 to 30th November 1948
46	1st November 1948 to 20th December 1948
48	1st November 1948 to 8th November 1948
52	1st September 1948 to 6th September 1948
53	1st July 1948 to 31st July 1948
54	1st September 1948 to 6th September 1948
58	1st November 1948 to 20th December 1948

Engineers found another use for 'Diddlers' at depots where they were allocated for training duties; rather than take a breakdown wagon or another trolleybus, they would use one to attend to disabled vehicles - the Highgate one ventured to Parliament Hill Fields on one occasion.

Decrepit is an appropriate word for Diddler number 7 - its nearside front mudguard is crumpled. It is in Station Road, West Croydon during its time as a training vehicle. Once 7's driver has passed his test he will be driving vehicles such as P1 1720 which is approaching the 630 West Croydon terminus; the destination blind is already set for NR WILLESDEN JUNCTION. Both trolleybuses are allocated to Hammersmith depot. *Don Jones*

An extension was made to the Stanley Road end of the depot after the last trams had departed; the new docking area enabled ten trolleybuses to be parked over pits. Q1s 1795 and 1800 await attention. *W. J. Haynes*

Bill Haynes was an official of London Transport and therefore it was relatively easy for him to get photographs on their property; he visited Fulwell depot one day and obtained a number of views of 1820, which are shown on this and the following page. The first is a good profile of a Q1. The second shows a fitter checking trolley booms while the last is from and of the roof showing the trolley gantry and booms to good effect. Whether it was the photographer or a member of staff who took this image is not known but it gives a good panoramic view of the maintenance area. *W. J. Haynes*

Lumbered with many of Highgate's down-trodden L3s on 1st February 1961, Fulwell's staff made a concerted effort to spruce them up; 1390 was one such vehicle. 1477, which came from Finchley on 7th November, was in a far better condition when it arrived here. With the arrival of L3s from Highgate there was an immediate uproar from drivers about how draughty the cabs were. Plates were fitted over both windscreen ventilators as seen on 1390. When more L3s came from Finchley in November they also had these plates fitted as seen on 1477.

Bill Legge

Fulwell was used during the conversion programme to store withdrawn vehicles; between stages seven and eight, 667, 657, 1273, 678 and 1279 are some of the 'unfortunates'; 657, 1273 and 1279 are from the Hammersmith 'stable'. Hanwell's 667 would have lasted longer had it not been for 780 hitting it up the back in Fulham Palace Road on 19th July 1960; F1 678 is also ex Hanwell. All these vehicles were sold to Cohen's in 1960. *Tony Belton*

1769 heads a line-up of Q1s inside the depot in January 1961; it had been delicensed after the Hanwell conversion and stored here for almost two months before being relicensed for 31 days (all of January). 1769 retains its HL code; either the painter has yet to paint FW on, or knowing its return to service will be short, has not amended it. 1769 was withdrawn on the night of 31st January/1st February 1961 and sent to Carballo in Spain where it was run into the ground for the next ten years. *Fred Ivey*

Having sat quietly in Fulwell Works for just over a month, 1218 (ex-Stamford Hill) and 1315 (ex-Edmonton) are outside the building at 8.05pm on Sunday 20th August 1961. The next morning they will leave the Stanley Road entrance and be driven via routes 601, 667 and 666 to a scrapyard in North West London – Colindale, a name most of London's trolleybuses feared! Note the original LUT road numbers displayed on the building: 1-10 for the depot with 11-15 for the works.
Tony Belton

Fulwell received many 'rough' L3s from Highgate depot at stage nine of the conversion scheme; the worst were replaced at stage twelve by far better L3s from Finchley. On page 252 mention is made of the cab ventilators being plated over; somehow 1422 has been missed. Deposed at stage twelve, 1422 and 1439 will leave for Colindale scrapyard on 15th December 1961.
Bill Legge

This view captures the famous Wellington Road end of the depot. 1504 has run in, 1514 is about to take up service and 1390 awaits a crew. Ivy no longer climbs up the depot walls.
Peter Moore

The driver has moved L3 1430 out of the depot and changed the trolley arms onto the wires that lead to Hampton Court. The white paint on traction poles at both ends of the depot was of greater height than at any other location.
Peter Moore

Number 1 was returned to Fulwell in March 1962; passing it as roadworthy enabled it to participate in a last day commemorative run on 8th May. It is seen shortly before this in front of the Works where it was stored for most of the intervening period. It has been driven out of Road 12; inside Road 11 is a withdrawn Stonebridge vehicle. Parked in front of the now closed Works are an RT, RM, RF and RFW. *Mike Beamish*

A photographic survey of the depot would not be complete without a last day shot. 1523, on route 605, enters in the evening of 8th May 1962; it has just about one more minute of life as further down the yard its trolley booms will be pulled down for the last time. A number of enthusiasts gather, both male and female. To the left a number of traction poles are piled; they will not be used in London again. *Mike Abbott*

STAFF TROLLEYBUS JOURNEYS

FULWELL   Routes 601, 603, 604, 667

	Nights of Sun/Mon to Fri/Sat.						Night of Sat/Sun.					
	601	601	601	601	601	601	601	601	601	601	601	601
Twickenham Junction		12. 7	1.15		4.11	5.21		12. 7	1.15		5.35	5.46
Fulwell Depot		12.14		3.10	4.18	5.28		12.14		4.33	5.42	
Stanley Road												
Wellington Road												
Hampton Court			1.34						1.34			
Kingston (Eden Street)		12.31	1.43	3.27	4.35	5.45		12.31	1.43	4.50		6. 3
Loop via Richmond Road and Kings Road												
Kingston (Eden Street)		12.44	1.56	3.39	4.48	5.58		12.44	1.56	5. 3		6.16
Hampton Court		12.53		3.48	4.57			12.53		5.12		
Wellington Road												
Stanley Road												
Fulwell Depot	11.58	1. 5	2.13	4. 0	5. 9	6.16	11.58	1. 5	2.13			6.33
Twickenham Junction	12. 5	1.12		4. 7	5.16	6.23	12. 5	1.12		5.31		

TROLLEYBUS ROUTES

TOLWORTH, Kingston By-Pass — SURBITON — KINGSTON — TEDDINGTON — TWICKENHAM

Via Warren Drive, Ewell Road, St. Marks Hill, Claremont Road, Penrhyn Road, Eden Street, Clarence Street, Kingston Bridge, Hampton Wick High Street, Kingston Road, Ferry Road, High Street Teddington, Broad St., Stanley Rd., Hampton Rd., The Green, Heath Rd., King St.

601

RAILWAY STATIONS SERVED: Surbiton, Hampton Wick, Fulwell   Service interval 5-12 minutes. Through fare 7d.

	MONDAY to FRIDAY		SATURDAY		SUNDAY	
	First	Last	First	Last	First	Last
TOLWORTH, Kingston By-Pass	6 10 6 40	1054 1223	6 19 6 49	11 7 1233	9 25	11 4 1233
SURBITON STATION	6 20 6 50	11 4 1233	6 21 6 27 6 58	1115 1241	8 57 9 34	1113 1241
KINGSTON, Eden Street	6 21 6 28 6 58	1113 1241	6 31 6 37 7 8	1124 1250	9 7 9 43	1123 1250
TEDDINGTON, St. Albans Church	6 31 6 39 7 8	1123 1250	6 15 6 38 6 45 7 16	1131 1256	8 51 9 14 9 50	1130 1256
FULWELL DEPOT	6 15 6 38 6 46 7 15	1130 1256	6 22 6 45 6 52 7 23	1138 †	8 58 9 21 9 57	1137 †
TWICKENHAM, King Street	6 22 6 45 6 53 7 22	1137 †				
TWICKENHAM, King Street	6 24 6 40	1140	6 24 6 42	1140	9 1	1140
FULWELL DEPOT	5 22 5 38 6 31 6 47	1147	5 19 5 36 6 31 6 49	1147	8 21 8 32 9 8	1147
TEDDINGTON, St. Albans Church	5 28 5 44 6 38 6 54	1154	5 25 5 42 6 38 6 57	1154	8 28 8 39 9 15	1154
KINGSTON, Eden Street	5 37 5 53 6 48 7 4	12 4	5 34 5 51 6 48 7 7	12 4	8 38 8 49 9 24	12 4
SURBITON STATION	5 44 6 0 6 56 7 12	1213	5 42 5 59 6 56 7 14	1213	8 46 8 58 9 32	1213
TOLWORTH, Kingston By-Pass	5 55 6 10 7 7 7 22	1223	5 53 6 9 7 7 25	1223	8 56 9 8 9 41	1223

† — Runs through to Twickenham as Staff Bus.

The above item is from a pre-war timetable.

MEMORANDUM	TO
OFFICE OF THE	
GENERAL MANAGER	THE CHAIRMAN

OUR REFERENCE	YOUR REFERENCE	
D/		DATE 9th August, 1945

The question of the replacement of the original 60 trolleybuses serving the old London United Tram area was left for further consideration, following the discussion at your meeting on the 26th July.

These trolleybuses were designed in 1931 and are now at a disadvantage as compared with the later types as they are inefficient and uneconomical. The incidence of failure of these vehicles is 5 times as great as that on the 1630 standard type trolleybuses, and their breakdown is a source of considerable inconvenience to the public. They were designed to operate on 500 volts, whereas the actual supply is about 600 volts, but apart from that mechanical defects have developed in the equipments. There are as many failures on the motors of these 60 vehicles as on the whole of the remainder of the fleet.

The bodies are of wooden construction and they were never sound and had to be rebuilt in 1935. They are again giving trouble owing to the original design, and if they are not replaced another rebuilding programme will have to be undertaken.

The seating capacity of the 60 trolleybuses is 56 as compared with the standard 70 seater vehicle, and to provide the same number of seats 51 vehicles would suffice.

We are, however, short of trolleybuses, and I would suggest that the full number should be ordered so as to provide a margin. There can be no question but that if a replacement is not to be carried out in the very near future we shall be faced with heavy expenditure on body repairs and re-wiring, which would not be satisfactory as it would still leave us with electrical and brake equipments which require much too frequent overhaul.

We are being pressed by the M.W.T. to give a decision upon this replacement question, as the number of new trolleybuses likely to be available in 1946 is small.

T.E. Thomas

T/610/2(3)
(5000 8/39)   MTM.

THE OLDEST TO THE NEWEST

Compared with the old LUT trams the 'Diddlers' were an instant hit with the travelling public, resulting in a big up-turn in traffic receipts. Operationally and from an engineering standpoint they proved disappointing and many modifications were made to them in their early days; they continued to be expensive to operate for the whole of their lives. When number 27 was photographed at Norbiton Church in the first half of 1933 it had already received attention from the resourceful Fulwell coachmakers; modifications to its bodywork included additional pillars at the front of the upper deck and strengthening brackets at the foot of the windscreen. Choke coils are now visible on the roof to counter radio interference. The overhead wiring (including the unconnected and seldom-used 'round-the-corner' facility) is constructed to 18 inch gauge; it was later re-hung to 24 inch specification in line with the rest of the London Transport system. Number 27 is working on route 3 to Tolworth. *George Bullock, courtesy Roger Monk*

The Fulwell engineering staff were no strangers to demonstration trolleybuses of which there had been three in 1930/31. Each had stayed for only a short duration but AHX 801, which came on loan from AEC in 1933, was destined to become a long-term feature of the Kingston area trolleybus network. Carrying London United fleetnames it entered service on route 4 on 27th March 1933 and was photographed soon afterwards at the Hampton Court terminus with an LT class six-wheeler bus passing by. This intriguing vehicle was still with London United when its assets passed to the London Passenger Transport Board on 1st July 1933. With underfloor mounted traction motor permitting a full-fronted body design seating seventy four, it instantly rendered the 'Diddlers' outdated in styling, carrying capacity and performance. Purchased by London Transport in March 1934 it became 61 in the trolleybus fleet and lasted in passenger service for the next seventeen years. This vehicle carried the classification A3 under the staircase from the early years of the war until withdrawal.

George Bullock, courtesy Roger Monk

Once London Transport had decided to replace their trams by trolleybuses no time was lost ordering two prototypes. A four-wheeler numbered 63 was delivered in August 1934; a six wheeler, number 62, arrived in July 1934. The pair soon entered service at Fulwell and were regulars on route 4 between Hampton Court and Wimbledon. With passenger capacity on 62 being seventy-three as opposed to sixty on 63 a decision was made for the three axle seventy seater to be standard for the fleet. 63 became a general dogsbody and was used for driver training and testing on various parts of the system; it came back to Fulwell in due course. With the arrival of Q1s in 1948 number 62 spent a few days at Walthamstow who within five days got rid of it to Holloway from where it was withdrawn in September 1952. Number 63 went to Hounslow where it stayed serviceable until 31st May 1952. In the immediate post war period both are seen at Hampton Court; 62, still with wartime white painted front mudguards, is on the 667. By now 63 has its third front blind format. It has blinds that could only be used on this vehicle. It is on route 604; as it is only going to Malden there is no option but to use a 605 display - there are no separate route and destination blinds so staff are only able to use a limited number of displays. When 63 was altered from half-cab to full-cab layout, the nearside front window became a one-piece affair rather than a split windscreen.

W. J. Haynes

An interesting vehicle purchased by London Transport was number 1671 which was a chassisless Leyland demonstrator. It had a Lancastrian registration number - DTD 649. It had four wheels at the front and two at the back, making it in appearance unlike any other London trolleybus. It had a seventy-seater body though the layout in the lower deck was different to a standard vehicle. The position for the step for the driver to get into the cab is awkwardly situated. 1671 was purchased on 19th September 1939 and given the fleet number 1671 with a classifcation of X7. It was allocated to Fulwell but, with the arrival of the first batch of Q1s, was sent to Hanwell in September 1948. It worked on routes 607 and 655 until withdrawal on 7th May 1955. Note the white paint on 1671's front mudguards and the traction standard. *W. J. Haynes*

The C1s sent to Fulwell in October 1935 were primarily for route 667. By the end of hostilities in 1945, the Diddlers were far from being reliable and when shortages occurred C1s would be pressed into service. This has happened on 26th May 1947 with 174 being seen at Wimbledon Town Hall taking on passengers for a trip on route 604 to Hampton Court. Although fitted with sidelights either side of its front panel it still retains its original police lights above the cab, though these are not used now. Also retained is the conductor's rear signalling window though this is now not used. Note how busy Wimbledon is. *Don Thompson*

All London Transport road passenger vehicles were given wartime external white markings so that they were visible to other road users at night. Although the Kingston area was not considered vulnerable Fulwell's Diddlers were not exempt from this sanction. At Tolworth 'Red Lion' A1 33 is parked on the 603 stand; PICTURE POST is prominently advertised. In early 1948 Q1s started to arrive and before long were operating on the Kingston routes; this embraced route 603 with 1792 seen on the same stand on 23rd April 1956. The Diddlers were gradually withdrawn with the last running towards the end of September 1948. For the previous few months both classes were operating alongside each other and it was common for a Q1 to follow a Diddler and vice versa. These views illustrate not only this possibility but how very different the two classes were – in fact the only similarity between them are two trolley booms.

W. J. Haynes/Peter Mitchell 8576

Then came the Q1s with the first batching arriving in 1948/1949. One of the later deliveries, 1828 is about to pass under the railway bridge in Heath Road, Twickenham on 27th May 1960. It is working on route 667 to Hampton Court; going the other way on the same service is 1832, whose conductor has not changed the rear destination blind. If an inspector saw two vehicles going in opposite directions both showing Hampton Court he would have strong words for the offender. These magnificent vehicles only saw service from three depots during their London lives – Fulwell, Hanwell and Isleworth. *Peter Mitchell 14668*

A second batch of Q1s, fifty in total, arrived in 1952/53. About a third were for Fulwell, with the rest going to Isleworth. Hardly had they been delivered than a number of the Isleworth trolleybuses moved to Hanwell. Over the years all of Fulwell's 1952 deliveries were to be seen at Hanwell for various lengths of time; however, 1842 was to spend more of its time at Fulwell than any of the others. It is seen passing through Hampton on route 667 to Hammersmith Broadway on 28th June 1959. Only two stages of the conversion programme have taken place and London Transport's avowed intention to keep the Fulwell and Isleworth routes operating until the late 1960s is still firmly in place. Within a year alternative plans were being made. *Peter Mitchell 13301*

The most powerful trolleybus in the fleet was Q1 1841 on account of its 125 horse-power motor; it was fitted with automatic acceleration but drivers were not endeared by this as it had a slow pick-up. Consequently, it spent much of its time over the pits in Fulwell depot where it is photographed. If Vernons Pools knew this they would have something to complain about. It went to Hanwell depot on 1st May 1958, spending eight months on the 607. It returned to Fulwell and was de-licensed on 1st June 1960. Ostensibly that was it but due to a number of F1s failing in the days before stage eight of the conversion programme, it was re-licensed to Hanwell in early November. It spent a few days back on the 607 and in fact was a very late runner on the last night. The body shell went to Cohen's, the motor and switch gear to the Imperial College Museum with the remainder of the units going into stock. *John L. Smith*

To replace the Q1s, a large number of L3s arrived in 1961 – first from Highgate and later from Finchley. Before being at Highgate 1392 was at West Ham; with both depots not being famed for looking after their vehicles it was not surprising that 1392 was one of many that only lasted nine months here. It was withdrawn after operations on 7th November 1961. Before this occurred 1392 is in Chiswick High Road by Netheravon Road on the approach to Youngs Corner on 7th August 1961 on route 667. *Peter Mitchell 18498*

Q1 1824

1824 was delivered to London Transport in June 1948; when this photograph was taken on 9th May 1953 in Richmond Road, Kingston on the 602, she was just under five years old and still looking good. The destination blind lacks a VIA in front of Surbiton – this was usual practice as Q1 blinds of the time were made at Chiswick Works not Aldenham.
Alan Cross

Coming towards the end of its days in London, 1824 is parked outside the redundant Savoy Cinema at Teddington. It is on the 605, a route it has worked on since 1948.
Fred Ivey.

Incredibly, and it is incredibly, 1824 was still available for service in December 1978, more than thirty years after it carried its first passengers. It was sold to Tranvia Electricos de Pontevedra in July 1961, becoming 101 in their fleet – it was the first to be adapted for righthand boarding, and one of three retaining open platforms throughout their lives in this small town. The workmanship of the Pontevedra staff was more than top class, the interiors of these vehicles being a literal mirror image of their time in London. The author and Caballeros (with the assistance of an English lady acting as a translator) spoke to the Pontevedra manager about purchasing 101 when he had finished with it. He wanted £1500 which in today's money is about £8,500 for a vehicle which was run into the ground, whose body frame was shot and which hadn't had a repaint for the whole time it was there. It had only cost £500 from London Transport plus shipping charges. Sadly no deal was made and the last that was heard of her was that she was going to be a camping vehicle. In October 1977 RT 3125 took a party of 'gricers' to see the remaining Q1s in Coruna and Pontevedra where 101 (which turned out to be the last Q1 in the town) was still plying its trade between Pontevedra and Marin; the photograph was taken on this trip. The fact that none of the Pontevedra Q1s had a repaint is illustrated by red paint showing through the cream paint on 1824's roof. On 14th April 1978, a Pontevedra driver allowed the author to drive 101 for most of the light running trip from Marin to the depot late at night. Maria, the conductress, was dropped off at Estribela and would pay the takings in the next day. Using the trolley retriever equipment, the author changed the poles from the mainline wires to the wires to the depot. He had been inspired to do this because Tony Belton had driven 105 from Marin to the depot the previous evening.   *Steve Lewis*

9.6.41

28.9.42

NOTES
The destination of HAMMERSMITH BDY is in the same height lettering as the via points. Note that the blind opposite just shows HAMMERSMITH and that many displays are in a different order to this one. A 601A display was never produced on Diddler blinds.

NOTES
There is no PRIVATE display; much linen has been saved by reducing some panels, e.g. there is only one reference to routes 602 and 603 rather than two. Neither blind has a Brentford Half Acre display. Blind material could have been saved by just using one instance of KEW BRIDGE.

PRIVATE TO HIRE A BUS APPLY 55 BROADWAY SW1 ABBEY 1234	KINGSTON **TEDDINGTON** (SAVOY)	PRIVATE TO HIRE A BUS OR COACH APPLY: 55 BROADWAY S.W.1 ABBEY 5600	VIA KINGSTON **MALDEN**
TEDDINGTON KINGSTON **TOLWORTH**	BRENTFORD TWICKENHAM **HAMPTON COURT**	TEDDINGTON KINGSTON **TOLWORTH**	VIA KINGSTON **TEDDINGTON** POST OFFICE
KINGSTON TEDDINGTON **TWICKENHAM**	TWICKENHAM BRENTFORD **HAMMERSMITH BDY**	KINGSTON TEDDINGTON **TWICKENHAM**	**WIMBLEDON** VIA TEDDINGTON
SURBITON **THE DITTONS**	**TWICKENHAM**	VIA SURBITON **THE DITTONS**	**TWICKENHAM** VIA TEDDINGTON
RICHMOND PARK KINGSTON GATE VIA LONDON ROAD	**BRENTFORD** (HALF ACRE)	**RICHMOND PARK** KINGSTON GATE VIA LONDON ROAD	BRENTFORD TWICKENHAM **HAMPTON COURT**
RICHMOND PARK KINGSTON GATE VIA RICHMOND ROAD	CHISWICK **KEW BRIDGE**	**RICHMOND PARK** KINGSTON GATE VIA RICHMOND ROAD	TWICKENHAM BRENTFORD **HAMMERSMITH BDY**
SURBITON **TOLWORTH** (RED LION)	BRENTFORD **KEW BRIDGE** *Alt	VIA SURBITON **TOLWORTH** RED LION	**TWICKENHAM**
FULWELL L.T. DEPOT VIA TEDDINGTON	BRENTFORD CHISWICK **SHEPHERDS BUSH**	**FULWELL** **DEPOT** VIA TEDDINGTON	**BRENTFORD** HALF ACRE
SURBITON **STATION**	CHISWICK BRENTFORD **HOUNSLOW**	**SURBITON** **STATION**	**KEW** **BRIDGE**
FULWELL **L.T. DEPOT**	ISLEWORTH **L.T. DEPOT**	**FULWELL** **DEPOT**	**STAMFORD BROOK** **STATION**
KINGSTON	*Alternative Format: **KEW** **BRIDGE**	**KINGSTON**	BRENTFORD CHISWICK **SHEPHERDS BUSH**
KINGSTON MALDEN **WIMBLEDON**		**FULWELL** **DEPOT** VIA HAMPTON COURT	CHISWICK BRENTFORD **HOUNSLOW**
MALDEN KINGSTON **HAMPTON COURT**		KINGSTON MALDEN **WIMBLEDON**	**ISLEWORTH** **DEPOT**
KINGSTON **MALDEN**		MALDEN KINGSTON **HAMPTON COURT**	

NOTE
This is a facsimile of a Q1 blind made at Chiswick Works in 1951. The only questionable panel is KEW BRIDGE as no photograph has been found with this display.

20.2.61

EXTRA
601
602
603
604
605
667
657

8.9.50

EXTRA
601
602
603
604
605
657
667

1.8.61

These were the last trolleybus route blinds manufactured.

EXTRA
601
602
603
604
605
657
667

26.3.52

PRIVATE
TO HIRE A BUS
APPLY. 55 BROADWAY S.W.I.
ABBEY. 1234

601
TEDDINGTON
HAMPTON WICK
KINGSTON
SURBITON STN

602
EDEN STREET
SURBITON STN

603
EDEN STREET
SURBITON STN
EWELL ROAD

604
RAYNES PARK
MALDEN
NORBITON
KINGSTON

605
MALDEN
NORBITON
KINGSTON
HAMPTON WICK

667
CHISWICK
KEW BRIDGE
TWICKENHAM
HAMPTON

657
CHISWICK
KEW BRIDGE
BUSCH CORNER
ISLEWORTH STN

17.8.51

601
TEDDINGTON
HAMPTON WICK
KINGSTON
SURBITON

602
PARK ROAD
EDEN STREET
PENRHYN ROAD
SURBITON

603
604
RAYNES PARK
MALDEN
NORBITON
KINGSTON

605
MALDEN
NORBITON
KINGSTON
HAMPTON WICK

667
CHISWICK
KEW BRIDGE
TWICKENHAM
HAMPTON

657
CHISWICK
KEW BRIDGE
BUSCH CORNER
ISLEWORTH STN

19.10.61

602/603 details combined as one panel to save material. Not only were these the last side blinds made but they were the last trolleybus ones of all to be manufactured.

ISLEWORTH (née HOUNSLOW)

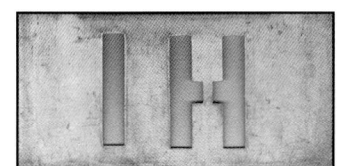

Opened 27th October 1935. Initially, partial operation was from a yard next to the depot which was the first to be converted from tram to trolleybus operation in one fell swoop. The only wartime incident of any significance occurred on 13th October 1940 when ten vehicles were slightly damaged. Re-named Isleworth on 12th July 1950.
It was the only depot to have permanent allocations of all three types: AEC, BUT and Leyland.

Closed to trolleybuses on 8th May 1962.
Routes operated: 657, 667 specials.
Type used: AEC, BUT and Leyland.
Capacity under cover was 37.
Number of vehicles licensed in March 1951 was 30.
Last trolleybus into depot: 1274 - route 657.

The LUT have placed advertising material on the boundary wall of the depot; wrought iron gates can be drawn across the entrance at any time as seen in this May 1927 view. Just one line of track suffices for entry and exit.
London Transport Museum U15885

Taken just a few days before the depot opened for trolleybuses, C1s 147 and 157 show a 604 route number implying some use at Fulwell with whom Hounslow had joint blinds. 157 is either moving on or off the traverser but work still needs to be carried out in the pit area to make it accessible. Guide rails are fitted to the pit in front of which 157 stands; this measure prevents any wheels running into it. The pit to the left has not yet had this feature added. In the background the office block is still being built. During the upheaval, trams on route 57 worked from the western side of the depot; trolleybuses are here for staff familiarisation.

London Transport Museum U18705

Some time before the first stage of their tram to trolleybus conversion - 27th October 1935 - London Transport became aware that Hounslow depot would not be ready in time for the opening. This was a high profile event with the 'eyes of the world' on it – the date just could not be put back. A yard to the east of the depot was seen as a solution. A surface strong enough to take the weight of a number of trolleybuses was laid and traction poles and wires erected; trolleybuses could head east and west from the yard. Those entering the yard did so on their traction batteries. C1 156 has left the yard and is ready to go to Hounslow; 156 is not the first vehicle out on the 657 (that was 147 at 7.49am) so the photograph was taken at a time when officials were out of their beds! Note the many bikes and the man working up a ladder. Vehicles that leave the yard for Hounslow need their trolley arms swung from the dead-ender to the main line wires. This indicates that this wiring layout will be there for quite a time. Another 657 leaves the yard for Hounslow; a further vehicle is inside the depot itself. Two STOP BY REQUEST signs have been erected. A second C1 leaves the yard. *London Transport Museum U18520*

273

136 (on the left) and 133 are seen in December 1936. It was a unique situation in that the offices and canteen were in the centre of the depot; trolleybuses parked either side. The many bicycles in the racks imply that staff come from a wide catchment area. *London Transport Museum U21382*

This view was taken on 21st October 1936, a year after the depot opened. C1s 151, 154 and 137 are over the pits awaiting attention; the 657 route numerals have a more curved feature than in later years. The top of the traverser is wooden planking. A short bamboo pole lies on the right-hand side of the traverser; these sawn-off poles were used to retrieve errant trolley booms which would only lift as far as the girders. Looking across the turntable and outside the stores, which seem bereft of any kind of spares, are three rear detachable metal mudguard sections. 151 and 154, which were bodied by Metro Cammell, have an offside conductor's signalling window, Weymann-bodied 137 does not. All vehicles are lavishly adorned with rear adverts; use in the corner positions generally ceased about 1938, though a few examples were to be found later than this.

London Transport Museum U21738

149, 144 and a third C1 are parked over the pits; 142 is ready to leave the traverser. A fitter attends to the heads of 144; a couple of employees are at their benches. The recess in the traverser pit gave access to its working parts. Hounslow was the first to have a turntable/traverser installed. *London Transport Museum U21387*

Isleworth was the only depot to operate the three types of trolleybus used by London Transport. First were AECs such as C1 155 which is parked at the exit in the days before code plates were introduced; it retains its front sidelights in their original position – the lights are yet to be positioned below the windscreen. HOUNSLOW DEPOT, shown on 155's front blind, is still the official name of this building. *Fred Reynolds*

Then came the BUTs with Isleworth having the highest numbered ones of the second batch. They were replaced in January 1961 by members of the initial batch as the newer ones were going to Spain first. Representing the Q1 era are 1814 which is leaving on an afternoon trip to Brentford Half Acre and 1831. Both were shipped to Vigo for re-use but in 1969 became marooned in the erstwhile tram depot and stayed there until early 1977 when they were broken up. Neither had carried a passenger since 25th April 1961; they lay dormant in Spain longer than they had run in London. Courtesy, Roger Rettig the cab door of 1814 was repatriated to Britain. *Peter Moore*

1060 and 1104 are both Leylands which was the last type to operate here; these two were considered to be amongst the best when selections were made at Wood Green as to which vehicles should hold up the final year of trolleybus operation of route 657. Note the different printing styles in the route and destination blinds on the two vehicles. Both were in service on Tuesday 8th May 1962. In fact 1104 was IH 8 which was 'last one in' on the Monday to Friday schedule – however, a gaily decorated 1274 took over the last round trip. *Peter Moore*

Shortly before Isleworth finished with Q1s, 1832 is parked over a wide pit on the west side of the depot. It is assumed it was widened when 8 foot wide Q1s replaced narrower C1s. *Peter Moore*

(b). Isleworth Trolleybus Depot - modifications to enable 8 gt. wide Trolleybuses to be operated. W & B.E.Est.B.5221. £163. To permit operation of 8 ft. Trolleybuses from Isleworth, certain alterations are required to dock pits and to the channel iron which forms a guide alongside the inspection pit. At present there is insufficient width between the pit proper and the sunken area to provide a safe margin when running a vehicle over the pit, and it may foul the gantry if the channel iron is not modified. APPROVED:

LIKE father, like son—that is how it has been with driver Harry Reeve, 56, of Isleworth trolleybus depot. Father George was also a driver—of horse-trams out of Jews Row, Battersea, more than 40 years ago.

Harry's most amusing experience (although not so at the time!) happened at Shepherds Bush when the trolleys of his bus came off the wires. There

(Concluded from page 18)

was a short delay while they were levered back. On to Chiswick Lane, where the bus stopped again, this time with one trolley off.

Harry got out of his cab and saw the reason why: they had been connected to the wrong overhead wires, and the bus had journeyed three miles with them crossed one over the other.

'Like father, like son' article is from a London Transport Magazine.

1107 has been cleaned and parked for the night. The route blind is from a Hanwell vehicle because some Q1s withdrawn at stage eight of the conversion scheme found themselves at Isleworth in the Q1 Merry Go Round movements in January 1961. Isleworth retained side and route blinds which incorporated 657 displays in case they were needed - they were. There was a total of twenty five Hanwell blinds in the Isleworth trolleybuses in 1962. In fact four vehicles - 1061, 1107, 1118 and 1146 were fitted throughout with Hanwell route and side blinds. This information was gleaned by the author winding through all the blinds on Saturday evenings. *Terry Cooper*

Shaw of Isleworth skies his trolleys on leaving the depot on Saturday 28th April 1962. In the top photo he has jumped out of the cab and makes a move towards the rear of 1126; meanwhile his conductor is about to put his right foot onto the roadway, his eyes looking towards the holder under the vehicle in which a bamboo pole is stored. In the lower view Shaw looks on disconsolately while his conductor gets to work with the bamboo. All dewirements were supposed to be reported - this one definitely wasn't! Shaw, who was the last man to pass his test as a London trolleybus driver and issued with badge T14876, said to the photographer "Don't let my guv'nor see that". Terry, it's well over fifty years on now and London Transport won't be knocking on your door as a result of your speed out of the depot that morning: so here it is!

Hugh Taylor

REPORT OF DEWIREMENT

Number	
Cause (agreed)	
District	
Divisional	
T.C.E.D.C.	

..................DEPOT..195......

Driver's name.. Badge number..........................
      (BLOCK letters)

Trolleybus number..................................... Time...................*a.m.
                                *p.m.

Length of delay to trolleybus concerned...............minutes. Route number...........................

Place of
dewirement (a) Name of road...(b) Pole number...............(c) Road *up/down

	Positive boom	Negative boom
Dewirement only—NO DAMAGE (If both booms dewired, enter "yes" in both columns)		
Was head twisted or damaged?		
Was head pulled off the boom?		
Did head, boom or part, fall to ground? If so, state which		
Was boom bent or broken?		

Suspected cause...

Estimated speed...........m.p.h. Was the trolley repaired on the road?.............. Was the trolleybus sent to depot?..............

Had you any previous trouble with the trolley?.............. Was the overhead equipment damaged?..............

If so, state damage..

Any other damage.............. (If "YES", Claims report must be submitted)   REPORT MUST BE CONTINUED ON OTHER SIDE

402/125
(20m 3/56-C16—Stock)   *Delete wording not applicable

A visitor to the depot on Sunday 29th April 1962 was Fulwell's 1528 (now the highest numbered trolleybus in the fleet). The top view sees it being turned on the traverser. Isleworth's short bamboo, which is covered in insulating tape, hangs from 1528's positive trolley arm. The lower photo sees Dick Bumstead at the traverser controls. The occasion is a tour by the Tramway Museum Society – weren't they the enemy of the trolleybus?
J.H.Price/Peter Moore

The photographer knew the last Q1s would be withdrawn at stage ten of the conversion programme; living locally he made a couple of forays to 657 territory in their final days. These photos were taken on Sunday 23rd April 1961 - there are just three more days of Q1 operation to go. The first view is the west bay; the second image is the east bay with 1789, 1765 and 1790 - the trio will be off to Spain later in the year with 1765 and 1789 operating in Coruna until January 1979. The third, 1790, only ran for about eighteen months – it was sold from Vigo to Coruna/Carballo and operated on their inter-urban route until March 1971. In the first photo is conductor Adrian O'Callaghan's car; behind is fitter Dick Bumstead's car which transported a number of Wood Green blinds to the author's home in early 1962. Dick lived at New Southgate and travelled all the way to Isleworth each day for work.

John Gillham

This sign was fitted at the entrance to the depot; pressing the bell the appropriate number of times meant that time was not lost identifying problems. It was the only depot to have an arrangement such as this. The young lad, Steve, is the photographer's son.
Don Lewis

RUNNING TO SCHEDULE

Good time keeping is the basis of good service.
Good service means that each vehicle receives a fair share of the day's work, and no man, driver or conductor, is doing the work of the other fellow.
When travelling at a speed of 30 miles per hour you cover 880 yards per minute. By running 30 seconds behind another Tram or Trolleybus at this speed you are 440 yards apart—quite a respectable distance. It will thus be seen why close poling is unnecessary apart from being dangerous. Inspectors are instructed to maintain even headways on each section of your route. You are asked to assist the Inspector in this work ; by doing this you will also assist your mates and the public.

Approved—
T. E. THOMAS,
General Manager,
London Passenger Transport Board,
55, Broadway, S.W.1.
24th December, 1943

T. J. TILSTON,
Operating Manager,
(Trams and Trolleybuses).

A 657 has run in one Saturday evening. In the picture are driver Goodridge, conductor Alan Buckland, fitter Bill Sumner and Hugh Taylor pulling its poles down.
Don Lewis

282

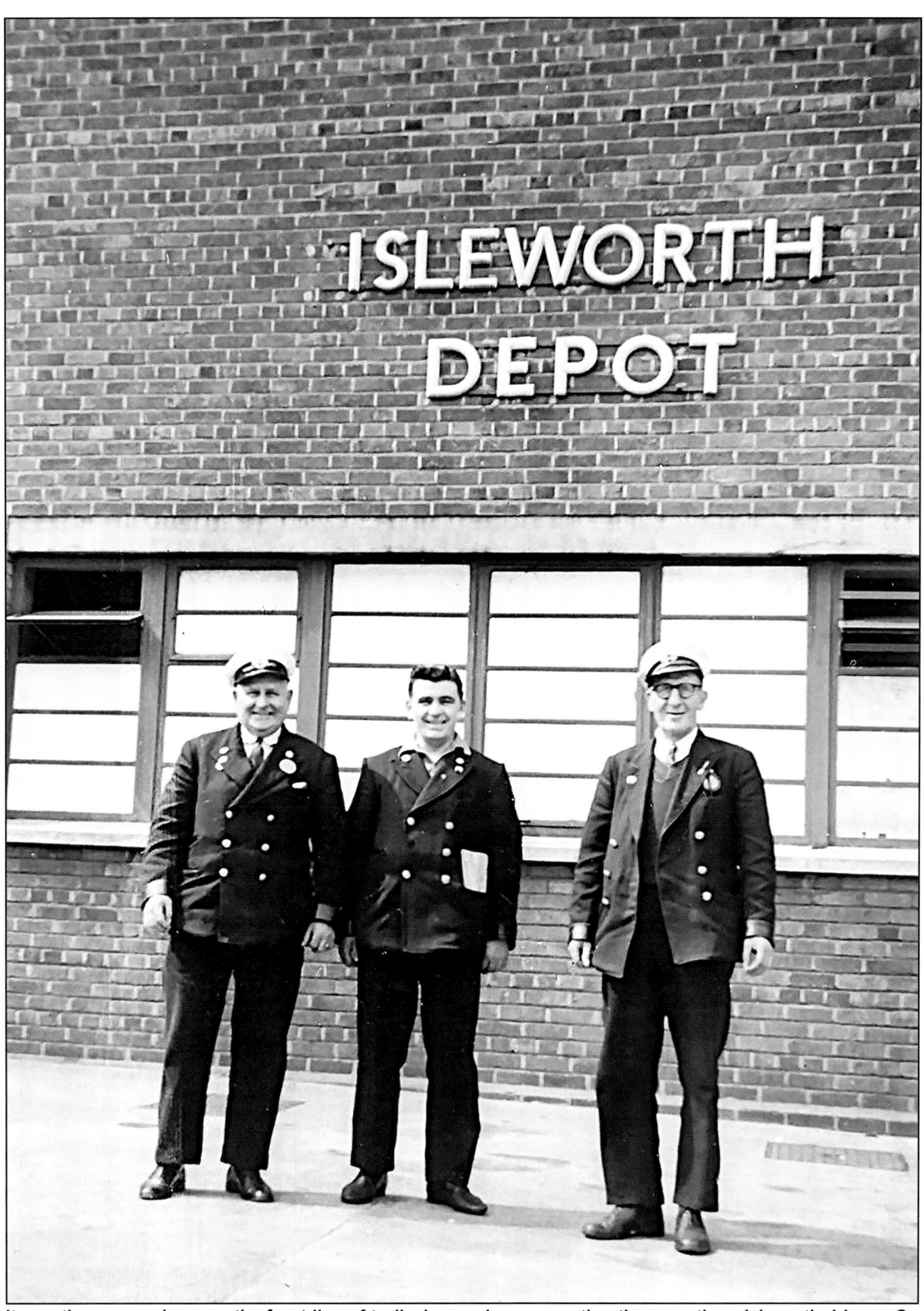

It was the crews who were the front-line of trolleybuswork; representing them are three Isleworth drivers. On the left is Fred Wakefield who drove Isleworth's last trolleybus (1274) to the depot on the night of 8th May 1962. Centre is Tony Shanny who dewired and bent 1116's negative boom at Busch Corner Brentford on the final morning (he still got it back to the depot). On the right is Len Watts who was also on duty that day.

A member of staff who took his camera to work one day

Isleworth maintenance staff are working hard on the final day of operation! It looks as if they have just finished decorating 1274's interior. Left to right are: Dick Bumstead; a relief man from Fulwell; Bill Sumner; the fitter known as 'Mickey Mouse', and a general hand. When Wood Green K1s were sent to Isleworth in April 1961, about half of them had RT moquette; the others had proper trolleybus moquette. 1274 was the last Leyland trolleybus to operate on the streets of Britain so it was fitting that she was attired with trolleybus moquette as can be seen here.

Hugh Taylor

1274's controller key; it was removed for safekeeping by the author on 12th May 1962 while the vehicle was sitting in Colindale scrapyard. Apart from a coloured light bulb, it is the only part of the last Leyland trolleybus that operated on the streets of Britain to survive.

Isleworth was going out in style. Considered to be the smartest, 1274 was set aside a few days before the depot closed so that staff could decorate her for the last journey on the night of 8th May 1962. That evening she waits for her special moment.

Peter Moore

```
                         TROLLEYBUSES
        Trolleybuses.                              Normal.

   Failure of Air Governor. T'bus 1875.  17.11.52.
   The C.M.E. referred to report on this incident from Mr.Shephard dated
   24.11.52., and was advised that an instruction had been issued for
   modification of the Governors;  22 out of 77 had been completed.  Mr.
   Schofield stated that he desired to examine the Governor of this
   particular vehicle, which had failed.

   It was noted that the matter had been referred to the Westinghouse Company,
   and the result of a meeting with them was awaited, it being understood
   that they would agree to effect a change.

   Reference was made to the fact that the air alarm on this particular
   vehicle was inoperative owing to the driver having jammed the time card
   between the warning flag and the air alarm body, thus preventing the
   warning signal being given of loss of air.   It had also been revealed that
   this was common practice on Q.1.vehicles at Isleworth, and suitable action
   had been taken by the Divisional Superintendent.

   Fractured Torque Blade - Trolleybus. (Min.636/11/52).
   Mr.Schofield stated that it was the present practice for all torque blades
   to be crack tested at overhaul.
```

1875 led a very mundane life during its time with London Transport. With Isleworth being a one-route depot, its daily routine was on route 657 between Hounslow and Shepherds Bush. It had a more varied life in Bilbao, Spain where it became number 875 in their fleet; the Q1s there worked on several routes. In 1958 there was a suggestion that the Q1s be fitted with flashing trafficators. It came to nothing. *Tony Belton*

Trolleybuses—Drivers' Cabins 17

Some drivers are making a practice of inserting spent matches and paper in the slot which houses the signal device fitted in the lower corner of the driving screen immediately to the left of the instrument panel and which projects a flag bearing the word "STOP" should the pressure on the brake gauge fall below 50 lbs.

This practice endangers the braking efficiency of the vehicle and in no circumstances should drivers make use of this slot as an ashtray or for the insertion of any foreign substance.

Traffic circular for 17th February 1956 - more than three years later this was still an issue.

TROLLEYBUSES OF THE 657

First to operate on the 657 were C1s. Still in reasonable condition in 1952 is 159 which has stopped just before the turning circle at Wellington Road, Hounslow. Its next trip will be to the depot for which it shows an intriguing blind panel. Hounslow was re-named Isleworth in July 1950 but this HOUNSLOW DEPOT display (paper style) was printed well after that date – another London Transport 'blind' anomaly. Very prominent on 159 is the position of the former route plate holder and the now out-of-use conductor's signalling window. *Fred Reynolds*

```
407/7/50. MANUFACTURE OF TRAM & TROLLEYBUS DESTINATION BLINDS. (Min. 370/7/50).
          Messrs. Bentall and Shephard reported favourably upon the paper blinds
          fitted to Trolleybuses at Hounslow in 1946 and at Fulwell in 1947, but
          submitted that white paper should be adopted and not blue.

          Mr. Bentall mentioned that a number of blinds manufactured by the silk
          screen process had been in service for too long a period and presented a
          shabby appearance.

          Since the production of paper blinds was more simple, economical and
          speedy, there appeared to be no justification for continuing with different
          types of blinds for buses and trolleybuses.  It was, therefore,

          DECIDED: (a) that white paper blinds be adopted for trolleybuses
                       and that the manufacture of blinds for both buses and
                       trolleybuses be concentrated at Aldenham; Mr. Ottaway
                       to plan accordingly.
                   (b) that the manufacture of blinds for trams by the silk screen
                       process be continued during their life.
```

Following the allocation of Q1s to Fulwell in early 1948 the three prototypes were re-allocated to other depots; two were kept in the former London United Tramways area - at Hounslow where X1 61 is outside the building before it was re-named Isleworth in July 1950. The date is deduced by the fact that 61 still has its original running number position. Judging by the footstep and the fact that the cab door opened differently to other trolleybuses, it must have been difficult for drivers to get into and out of the cab. Another idiosyncrasy was that special blinds had to be made for it (front, side and back). 61 came out of service on 31st May 1951, to spend the rest of its time (until 4th June 1952) as a designated training vehicle. X3 63 fared a little better in terms of passenger carrying days; it was last licensed on 31st May 1952. These vehicles often ran just between Hounslow and Brentford; not always though, and outside Hollygrove Ironworks (just before Hounslow terminus) 63 has its blind already set for Shepherds Bush. Both vehicles work on route 657, Isleworth being a depot that only operated one route.

Fred Reynolds/Brian Chaplin

During the time that 378 was allocated to Isleworth depot it is seen over the pits in the incoming road - Q1s will be arriving imminently as indicated by the words 'WIDE PIT'. An unidentified C1 is on the left - it has a Chiswick produced paper route blind while 378 has a Charlton manufactured linen one. *John Clarke*

As can be seen by its history card, 378 was passed from pillar to post. It spent exactly a year at Isleworth (1st June 1951 to 31st May 1952) working on route 657. It had been a pay-as-you-board experimental vehicle in 1946; its step entrance was unpopular with crews, hence its nomadic existence. *Brian Chaplin*

The next main class to be allocated to the 657 was the Q1 with 1886 seen west of Ashchurch Grove on Goldhawk Road on 30th July 1956 heading for Shepherds Bush. It was common for trolleybuses to advertise Ben Truman ale at this time. *Peter Mitchell 9233*

Holding up the 657 service for its last twelve months were a number of K1s transferred from Wood Green. These were chosen in preference to equally good conditioned K2s as the K1s' Metrovick electrical equipment was considered better than the K2s' English Electric equipment. London Transport used the K1s in preference to K2s as the electrical equipment of the former was the better of the two. Most came at stage ten of the conversion programme; a couple more arrived at stage twelve. It is Sunday 7th January 1962 and only Fulwell and Isleworth depots are sending trolleybuses onto the capital's streets now. It is a bleak day with all of 1058's windows closed. The few pedestrians are well wrapped up, with Shepherds Bush Green itself devoid of people. *Peter Mitchell 19771*

1060 has run into Isleworth depot during the evening of Saturday 21st April 1962; the author dropped its poles. It looks as if Jack Guy, on the left, is remonstrating with his colleague, nicknamed Mickey Mouse whose real name I never got to know. These two were forever having a tiff and each would say to me about the other "Silly old fool". I remained neutral and carried on with my work of dropping poles. By looking at the chit alongside it is possible that he is Mr Brent. 1060 shows 667 ISLEWORTH DEPOT; the author had wound up the route number to show this display as in times past Isleworth had operated on this route on Bank Holidays. *Hugh Taylor*

ISLEWORTH DEPOT LOG SHEET — DATE 31 MAR 1962
ROUTE NUMBER 657 VEHICLE NUMBER 1221 RUNNING NUMBER 9

Point	Arr. time	Dep. time	Point	Arr. time	Dep. time
Depot		9-17	Wellington	9.25	9.30
S Bush	10.10	10.12	"	10.52	10.58
"	11.38	11.40	"	12.20	12.26
"	16	18	"	1.48	1.54
"	2.34	2.36	"	3.16	3.22
SB	4.42	4.44	wL	4.44	4.50
SB	5.30	5.32	wL	6.12	6.18
DEP		6.26			

402/60 (5)
(1000m-6/61-D20-Stock)

ISLEWORTH	DAILY RECORD OF VEHICLES IN AND OUT				31 OCT 1961	
TIME	VEHICLE NO	DRIVER	AUTHORITY NO	PURPOSE OF JOURNEY FROM OR TO	CODE	MILES
2.30	1291	C/F PERRY	25.10.61 76084	TO FULWELL (SCRAP)	B33	—
1.30 / 2.00	1072	FITTER BRENT	27.10.61 76089	DEPOT - HALF ACRE	B9	5
4.30	1199	C/F WITTY	29.10.61 76088	TO HENDON (COHENS) SCRAP	B33	

291

The docket on the previous page is for three movements from Isleworth depot. Obviously there are no views of these but the two photographs above are the best that can be done. 1778 is having a test run between the depot and Half Acre and is in St Pauls Road, Brentford. 1072 passes through Busch Corner on a trip to Hounslow on the 657 - this is the way 1072 went on 27th October 1961. *Peter Moore/Tony Belton*

292

The docket on page 291 shows K2 1199 going to Colindale scrapyard. It details the trip to Hendon (Cohens) Scrap – this was the terminology used by the person entering the details. 1199 was mistakenly sent from Wood Green to Isleworth at stage ten of the conversion programme. It was one of thirty K1s that were transferred. 1199 arrived on the night of 25th/26th April 1961 and for the next six months just trundled up and down the east side of the building, getting in the way. However, an IH code was painted on and the 'Buses for Trolleybuses' route 629 poster on the nearside window was removed. This was all done in double quick time as shown in this view on 28th April. The question is whether it actually ran from Isleworth. It took six months before bureaucracy came to its senses - 1199 went for scrap on 29th October. This extensively delayed its dismantling. *Tony Wild*

The other vehicle named on the docket is 1291 which has run into something; judging by the amount of damage it must have been quite an impact. The collision occurred sometime towards the end of October 1961 - it was transferred to Fulwell on the 25th of the month. Why it was sent there is not known - it could have gone to the scrapyard directly from Isleworth. It is passing through Twickenham on its way to Colindale scrapyard on 3rd November. It is surprising that the driver is prepared to drive it for a lengthy journey with that amount of damage to the windscreen – surely his vision was impaired. Cohen's usually picked up damaged vehicles.
Fred Ivey

Isleworth had a hand painted blackboard with the times that running numbers ran in and ran out. The author copied the details into his notebook one Saturday evening and these are shown below.

MONDAY TO FRIDAY

Running Number	Time out a.m.	Time in a.m.	Running Number.	Time in p.m.
10	4.29		22	6.14
14	4.51		23	6.21
22	5.14	9.38	24	6.24
17	5.29	9.06	1	6.30
23	5.37	9.53	2	6.33
9	5.46		10	6.38
15	6.00	8.50	20	6.48
16	6.06	8.58	5	6.51
13	6.11		9	6.55
21	6.21	9.34	12	6.56
18	6.28	9.19	18	7.03
3	6.32		14	7.07
20	6.26	9.27	11	7.12
1	6.43		15	7.20
5	6.44		4	10.51
6	6.49		17	11.02
19	6.51	9.25	7	11.09
7	6.59		21	11.20
8	7.08		3	11.27
24	7.16	10.08	16	11.38
11	7.26		6	11.46
12	7.28		13	11.56
2	7.55		19	11.57
4	8.07		8	12.53

		SWINGS		
Running Number	Time in	Time out		
15	8.50	3.23		
16	8.58	3.34		
17	9.06	3.40		
18	9.19	3.45		
19	9.25	3.47		
20	9.27	3.52		
21	9.34	3.54		
22	9.38	4.02		
23	9.53	4.06		
24	10.08	4.12		

NB. SWINGS was the Isleworth terminology for the running numbers that came in to the depot after the morning peak hour and went out before the evening peak hour.

SATURDAY

Running number	Time out a.m.	Road number	Time In p.m.	Running number	Time in
3	4.29	3	6.03	20	5.40
10	4.51	3	12.58	1	5.45
14	5.12	2	11.12	3	6.03
18	5.29	3	7.03	5	6.09
21	5.43	2	11.42	7	6.18
5	6.06	3	6.09	9	6.26
6	6.13	3	11.51	11	6.33
12	6.33	2	11.04	13	6.41
15	6.48	2	10.58	16	6.56
19	7.03	2	11.13	18	7.03
1	7.17	4	5.54	15	10.58
8	7.46	4	11.58	12	11.04
17	8.18	4	11.27	14	11.12
20	8.31	1	5.40	19	11.13
22	8.39	1	11.28	17	11.27
2	8.46	1	11.57	22	11.28
4	8.54	1	11.43	21	11.42
7	9.09	4	6.18	4	11.43
9	9.17	1	6.26	6	11.51
11	9.24	3	6.33	2	11.57
13	9.32	3	6.41	8	11.58
16	9.43	3	6.56	10	12.58

SUNDAY

Running number	Time out a.m.	Time in p.m.	Running number	Time in
8	5.48	11.16	9	7.00
1	6.02	11.46	5	7.56
4	6.17	11.56	7	11.08
5	6.32	7.56	8	11.16
7	6.47	11.08	10	11.26
11	7.17	11.36	11	11.36
6	9.35	12.53	1	11.45
10	10.05	11.56	3	11.46
3	10.35	11.46	4	11.56
9	12.57pm	7.00	2	11.57
2	1.27pm	11.57	6	12.53

STAFF TROLLEYBUS JOURNEYS

ISLEWORTH   Route 657

	NIGHTS of Sun/Mon to Fri/Sat.			Night of Sat/Sun.	
	657	657		657	657
Hounslow		12.25			12.30
Isleworth Depot		12.33			12.38
Bush Corner		12.38			12.43
Brentford		12.41			12.46
Brentford		12.43			12.48
Bush Corner		12.48			12.53
Isleworth Depot	12.15	12.53		12.20	12.58
Hounslow	12.23			12.28	

Note that Busch Corner has been misspelt.

Blind 1	Blind 2	Blind 3	Blind 4
PRIVATE TO HIRE A BUS OR COACH APPLY: 55 BROADWAY S.W.I ABBEY 1234 TEDDINGTON KINGSTON **TOLWORTH** KINGSTON TEDDINGTON **TWICKENHAM** VIA SURBITON **THE DITTONS** **RICHMOND PARK** (KINGSTON GATE) VIA LONDON ROAD **RICHMOND PARK** (KINGSTON GATE) VIA RICHMOND ROAD VIA SURBITON **TOLWORTH** (RED LION) **FULWELL DEPOT** VIA TEDDINGTON **SURBITON STATION** **FULWELL DEPOT** **KINGSTON** **FULWELL DEPOT** VIA HAMPTON COURT KINGSTON MALDEN **WIMBLEDON**	MALDEN KINGSTON **HAMPTON COURT** VIA KINGSTON **MALDEN** VIA KINGSTON **TEDDINGTON** (SAVOY) BRENTFORD TWICKENHAM **HAMPTON COURT** TWICKENHAM BRENTFORD **HAMMERSMITH BDY** **TWICKENHAM** **BRENTFORD** (HALF ACRE) **KEW BRIDGE** GOLDHAWK ROAD **YOUNGS CORNER** BRENTFORD CHISWICK **SHEPHERDS BUSH** CHISWICK BRENTFORD **HOUNSLOW** **ISLEWORTH DEPOT**	TEDDINGTON HAMPTON WICK KINGSTON SURBITON EWELL ROAD PARK ROAD EDEN STREET PENRHYN RD SURBITON PORTSMOUTH RD PARK ROAD EDEN STREET PENRHYN RD SURBITON EWELL ROAD RAYNES PARK NEW MALDEN NORBITON KINGSTON HAMPTON CT RD HAMPTON WICK KINGSTON BDGE CLARENCE ST LONDON ROAD NORBITON	HAMPTON CT RD KINGSTON BDGE CLARENCE ST LONDON ROAD NORBITON CHISWICK KEW BRENTFORD TWICKENHAM HAMPTON HAMPTON TWICKENHAM BUSCH CORNER BRENTFORD KEW YOUNGS CORNER CHISWICK TURNHAM GREEN GUNNERSBURY STATION CHISWICK KEW BRENTFORD ISLEWORTH (SPRING GROVE)
17.8.56		12.1.44	

12.1.44
The (Spring Grove) qualifying point appears to be the only instance of brackets appearing on a side blind.

Fulwell and Isleworth had joint blinds. Initially these were stamped as Fulwell and Isleworth and latterly as FW and IH.

**EXTRA
607
655
667
657**

29.4.58

From January 1961 until May 1962, Isleworth used a lot of Hanwell route blinds which incorporated route 657.

It would be remiss not to include in this set of books the highest numbered vehicle in the London trolleybus fleet. 1891 is seen leaving Isleworth depot for Hounslow on the 657 in its last month of service to Londoners - January 1961. Always allocated to Isleworth, it did manage to operate from all three former London United Tramway depots. On 3rd February 1959, Fred Ivey noted it working on Hanwell's 607 route and, in the merry-go-round of movements at stage nine of the conversion programme, it spent its last days working at Fulwell depot. *Fred Ivey*

HANWELL

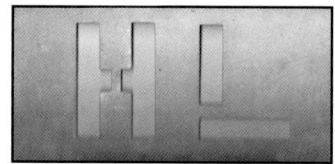

Opened 15th November 1936. Work on the depot was not complete at opening day so some of the allocation was worked by Acton depot until it became fully functional on 10th March 1937. It was the recipient of a German bomb on 23rd June 1944; no vehicles were badly damaged. A more serious incident occurred on 10th May 1940 when twenty-one were damaged.

Closed to trolleybuses on 8th November 1960.
Routes operated: 607, 628 (Bank Holidays), 630 (Bank Holidays), 655, 660, 666, 667 specials*
Type used: Leyland and BUT.
Capacity under cover was 108.
Number of vehicles licensed in March 1951 was 115.
Last trolleybus into depot: 1812 - route 607.

Though Hanwell only operated on route 667 on Bank Holidays, many arrangements had to be made for these workings. The destination blinds incorporated most 667 destinations. Fare tables had to be provided and special tickets produced which were only used a few times a year. Apart from any occasions when Fulwell's TIM machines broke down, this would be the only time passengers on route 667 received bell punch tickets. A traffic circular in this chapter details various matters about the 667 trips. Conductors sometimes showed EXTRA rather than 657 or 667.

This May 1927 view illustrates LUT cars 28 and 308; the latter has been on route 7A which worked between Southall and Shepherds Bush. Hanwell was not a large tram depot but it was anticipated that about a hundred trolleybuses needed to be housed. Consequently it became the most expensive to construct.
London Transport Museum H13545

It is 6th October 1936 and Hanwell trolleybus depot is in the course of construction; there is still a long way to go before it can be used. The work in converting Hanwell was so extensive that it was not completed in time for the anticipated conversion date and some of its allocation was temporarily worked by Acton depot. The LONDON UNITED TRAMWAYS LTD sign stayed on the central building until the end of tram operation; it was then cleared away to create a wide forecourt. Only a single track is available through the narrow entrance. J. Jarvis won the contract to adapt a number of tram depots for trolleybuses in the pre-war years; this was one.
London Transport Museum U21644

There was inconsistency with regard to names attached to trolleybus depots – some had no details at all. HANWELL TROLLEYBUS DEPOT is prominently displayed on the new administrative block; a LONDON TRANSPORT symbol is attached. To passers-by the depot must have looked a very modern looking building for its time. At the entrance on 12th May 1937 D2 414 shows 655 HANWELL BROADWAY; with the arrival of F1s it will soon go to Hammersmith depot. On this summer's day 'special work' casts a shadow on the roadway. By 1954, the HANWELL TROLLEYBUS DEPOT sign had been removed.
London Transport Museum U23899

Hanwell depot on 27th May 1937 with D2s 449 and 451 haphazardly positioned; 452 and 444 are parked more professionally - all have 'condiment' advertisements on their lower rear panels. Many vehicles are over the docking pits beyond the traverser; long lines of troughing are noticeable. In the foreground, hoses run from the roof enabling vehicles to be washed by hand. Two interesting vehicles are in view. 660 (delivered the previous month) is in the middle distance and facing the camera just in front of the washing gantries; it shows 667 HALF ACRE VIA CHISWICK, implying that blinds have just been put in. To the very right is the first F1 (number 654) which has been out on the road. F1s are starting to replace D2s; route 607 needed vehicles which could reach high speeds quickly - D2s were not powerful enough, hence the class change.

London Transport Museum U23900

Hanwell was a recipient of a German bomb on 23rd June 1944; despite the devastation to the premises no vehicles were seriously damaged – 693 is one that 'got away with it'. It is just a matter of clearing up and attending to vehicles before they go out again. A more serious incident had occurred on 10th May 1940 when twenty one vehicles were damaged, 672 and 727 so seriously that were very fortunate to survive; an enormous amount of money was spent repairing them.
London Transport Museum U33047/33048

The office block shows Hanwell again but it states HANWELL GARAGE - the sign has prematurely been placed on the building. 725 on route 607 approaches Hanwell trolleybus depot in its last days. The conductor will nip off the platform, pull the frog handle and 725 will be home again.
Tony Belton.

Diddler 15 was a training vehicle here between 9th November 1948 and 1st June 1949. It is parked adjacent to the Jessamine Road entrance with its poles down – whether it has finished its stint in this capacity or it is just having a rest is not known. Its rear has part of a SAXA advert pasted over a DUNLOP advert. CAPSTAN cigarettes are also promoted.
Don Jones

AEC 260 has been loaned from Stonebridge to Hanwell and has been out on the 607. Drivers will find it 'feels different' as Hanwell was a Leyland depot; if they have not driven an AEC before they will be unaccustomed to the reverser handle and controller key. 260 has a lower horse-power motor than the native F1s so may struggle to keep to time.

Don Jones

Another AEC to set foot in Hanwell depot was one of the N2s that Stonebridge used for training purposes -1658. Their drivers were unlikely to work from Hanwell so the reason for its visit would have been on the whim of the instructor who either liked the canteen or wanted to see a colleague there. 1658 turns right out of the depot to head east back towards home territory.

Tony Belton

677 has a fault of some description and its driver has arranged for a substitute to be made available at the depot. He has brought it onto the forecourt and passengers get on 1879 which will take its place in the 607 service. Both booms are almost at full stretch as an inspector places the positive boom on the overhead. It was uncommon for passengers to board vehicles in London Transport depots or garages, but needs must. Corrugated iron surmounts the inspectors' hut, implying that its wooden roof is leaking. *John Buckle*

There always seemed to be trolleybuses parked on the forecourt. It was the off-peak hour terminus of route 655; F1 721 illustrates this. Parked alongside is sister vehicle 693 which is out of service at present. *Tony Belton*

716 gleams and is a credit to the Fulwell overhaul staff; at Hanwell now it will be given a thorough check-over before going out on the road. A 'DONT MOVE' sign has been placed on the cab door; it does not say DO NOT MOVE or DON'T MOVE. 716 was released from overhaul on 9th July 1959, to be withdrawn just sixteen months later. In the background, steps lead to what is probably the foreman's office; a time clock and clocking-in cards are seen below it.
John L. Smith

Pausing from the daily slog one Sunday are H1 782 and F1 696. Most overhead in the parking lanes was 'dead-ended', only a few being joined to wires leading to the exit. 782 is in a lane in which there is no overhead; battery mode will need to be used to get it onto wires that lead out of the depot.
Tony Belton

To allow 655s to terminate at Hanwell Broadway on Sundays an entrance was made into the side of the depot; access was by terraced Jessamine Road. It was not ready when the route started on 13th December 1936 and journeys on the Sabbath had to turn on the loop outside Hanwell bus garage until March 1937. It is now near the end of trolleybus operation as a sign for BOOTH (contractors) is fixed to the depot wall. Always at Hanwell, F1 683 enters the building.
Peter Moore

Trolleybuses have been washed, cleaned and laid to rest after another day on West London streets. Left to right are F1 700, K2 1204 and H1 774; as the end approached Hanwell had various classes allocated with the hundred strong F1 greatly reduced in number. Not only did the cleaners deal with the interior and exterior of the vehicle but a daily task was to remove tickets from the USED TICKETS receptacle positioned below the Metropolitan Stage Carriage Licence plate.
Peter Moore

Seven trolleybuses are neatly positioned; the usual fare in 1960 was F1, K1, K2 and Q1 with examples of each in view. Hanging from a roof girder, a bamboo pole is in a handy position. All vehicles show HANWELL BROADWAY – five 607s and two 655s. Q1 1766 was the penultimate trolleybus to be overhauled by London Transport – the last the author saw of it was in the garden of the Coruna-Carballo's general manager!

Peter Moore

F1 740 and Q1 1844 are over the pits; the six inch width difference at the rear of the two classes is very noticeable. Overhead wires are anchored against roof girders; the traverser controller is prominent on the right. For most of its Q1 era, Hanwell used those from the second batch; Fulwell, the first recipients of these post-war vehicles, had all of the first batch, constructed four years earlier. On the left is breakdown tender 123A which belongs to Hanwell. On the right, a member of the engineering staff carries out some 'private' work – who does the car belong to and shouldn't he be doing something 'trolleybus'?

Tony Belton

MANY DIFFERENT CLASSES.

Hanwell got landed with some oddities of the trolleybus fleet with some re-bodied examples finding their way here in the post-war period; one was D2A 95A which had been lengthened as well getting a new body following war damage as B2 95. It is outside Ealing Common Station where a headway interval clock recorded the passage of westbound trolleybuses. The positive trolley head touched a skate on the overhead which sent an impulse to a clock (inside the station and at 55 Broadway, London Transport Headquarters) which went BOOOMF in the process. Heading for Shepherds Bush on route 607, in this mid-fifties view, 95A has all its windows closed. A British Railways advertisement is on the side - there are no adverts on the front. The backside of a horse and its milk float are to the right.

Peter Brazier, courtesy Bus of Yesteryear

At London Transport's HQ at 55 Broadway, London, SW1, six trolleybus headway clocks were open to full public view. The casing states the purpose of the instruments which is to indicate the number of trolleybuses passing six points each hour. Close inspection shows that the photograph was taken at about 3pm. The date is 12th May 1959. Note the Ealing Common clock on the left. *London Transport Museum U8807*

This photograph epitomises a trolleybus at rest. H1 774 operated from Hanwell depot from May until November 1960, having replaced an F1 that had fallen by the wayside. Much work is going on in preparing the building for its new role as a bus garage; rubble is dumped behind 774 - in front of it wooden doors have been removed. *Tony Belton*

An 'odd-bod' allocated to Hanwell for many years was D1 384, the only Leyland trolleybus with spats over its rear wheels; it is on Hayes End Road shunt ready for return to Shepherds Bush. Route 607 had a higher number of vehicles allocated to it than any other – seventy five at the time with 384 being HL 65. Again, British Railways advertise on the side of the vehicle but there are no takers for the front spots. The usual fare on the 607 were F1s – 711 is in the background.   *Fred Reynolds*

D2s were the first class allocated to Hanwell; however, they soon proved inadequate for the busy and frequent 607 service due to the low horse-power rating (80h.p) of the traction motor. 409, one of the earliest D2 deliveries, was photographed on 15th March 1936 at the Shepherds Bush terminus of the route; of note is the TROLLEYBUS STOP flag on the right. The 607 ran between Shepherds Bush and Uxbridge; the busiest section was between here and Southall so many journeys only went that far west. 409, still to half cab design, would find itself at Bexleyheath before long; it was an unfortunate victim of wartime bombing and upon re-bodying assumed a new fleet number. On page 335, it is illustrated as 409B.   *London Transport Museum U22312*

Unique in the fleet was four-wheel steering 1671 which is HL 2 in the 607 service; in the top photo it will be observed that the depot code plate is missing. In the first view it is on the north side of Shepherds Bush Common; soon it will proceed to the pick-up point on the other side of the triangle (Shepherds Bush Green) where it is seen in the lower image.
Fred Reynolds

The D2s were soon replaced by vehicles with more powerful motors: F1s with the hundred strong class remaining here until 1953 when service cuts saw some move to Highgate. These all-Leyland vehicles were so sound that ninety were still in service when 1960 came round. Route 655 was Hanwell's secondary route and on 21st March 1960, working on the peak hour extension to Clapham Junction, 684 is in Fulham Palace Road close to Colehill Lane which is to the immediate right. There was a short working point here; this was FULHAM PALACE RD EDGARLEY TERRACE. Vehicles used Edgarley Terrace, Firth Road and Colehill Lane for the manoeuvre. The trailing frog is from Colehill Lane. Behind, P1 1710 works on route 630 to West Croydon.
Peter Mitchell 14176

With the policy of retaining more recently overhauled vehicles in service as opposed to those that had been dealt with less recently, Hanwell's F1s started to be withdrawn in numbers at stage five of the conversion scheme (February 1960); they were replaced by Ks which gained a foothold thereafter. Illustrating this is K1 1152 at The Lawn, Shepherds Bush having just started its long journey to Uxbridge on the 607 in the late afternoon winter sunshine of Saturday 5th November 1960. Amongst other traffic, Q1 1874 on route 657 heads for the full length of its route – Hounslow.
Peter Mitchell 16642

On many Bank Holidays Hanwell operated an unadvertised 667 service between Shepherds Bush and Hampton Court with eleven vehicles which required nineteen duties. Crew reliefs were at Busch Corner with staff travelling to Isleworth depot for their meals. On Whit Monday 1960 (6th June) Q1 1846 is at the bottom of Goldhawk Road by Youngs Corner on its way to Hampton Court. 'Close-poling' 1846 is Isleworth's 1889 on the 657 to Hounslow; its conductor will have an easy time as far as Busch Corner where they will go their separate ways. S Collins & Sons, who are high class ladies and gents tailors, are closed for the day. Isleworth drivers knew they had to come out of Goldhawk Road into Chiswick High Road over a manhole cover - this 'marker' avoided a dewirement. Hanwell staff only came down the 657 wires occasionally and 1846's driver has not taken the right line with the result that the negative trolley arm has left the wire. The driver has left his cab door open while he re-poles his vehicle.

Tony Belton

Seventeen Q1s were to be withdrawn in November 1960; with maintenance on the majority of Hanwell's vehicles being reduced in the months preceding the conversion, sixteen of them came here in June 1960. Late running and subsequent curtailments were common on the 607; both 1772 and 1765 find themselves in this situation with their crews being instructed to curtail short of Uxbridge. 1765 has its 'sticks' down while 1772 is on the short-working wire, turning at STRATFORD BDG (bottom of Hillingdon Hill). Not only are they running late but have got themselves out of order; the crews rectify the situation. This short-working point needed trolleys swung to a dead-end wire as there was no facing frog to assist staff here. *Tony Belton*

Until early 1953 the most common class of trolleybus on route 607 were the F1s; before long they were joined by some Q1s. F1 715 and Q1 1849 are recognisable on the Uxbridge stand; the booms of a third vehicle can be discerned. This photograph was taken on 1st May 1960; by the end of June, 1849 and fifteen other Q1s were moved from Hanwell to Fulwell with sixteen of Fulwell's Q1s going the other way. The reason for this was to get the less recently overhauled Q1s to Hanwell where reduced maintenance was literally the order of the day for all of HL's trolleybuses. The reason for toning down Q1 maintenance was that they were due for withdrawal on the night of 8th November 1960. Note the different styling of UXBRIDGE on 1849's blind with that of 1164's opposite. 715 ended up in a pile of scrap at Colindale, London, NW9, while 1849 spent many a year as 849 in the Bilbao trolleybus fleet in Spain. *Tony Belton*

Uxbridge was the most westerly point reached by London trolleybuses and the outer terminus of London Transport's most prestigious trolleybus route – the 607. During its peak years, 607s were passing through Hanwell Broadway at one per minute during the busiest peak hours. Once past Southall and on dual carriageways the rest of the way, drivers would have their charges on top notch, with the result that it was not uncommon to find three on the stand at Fray's Bridge; this was one of many places where the trolleybuses had to be extended from the erstwhile tram routes. The 607 is best known for its F1s but in this instance K2 1164, Q1 1877 and K1 1154 occupy Uxbridge stand. The photograph has to have been taken after 26th July 1960 when 1164 was relicensed at Hanwell – F1s are starting to fall by the wayside now. 1154 would survive the Hanwell conversion and stay in service until November 1961 at Wood Green. 1164 would go for scrap at the Hanwell conversion with 1877 being withdrawn at this time too. 1877 was sold to Bilbao in Spain and converted into a wretched motorbus where it became number 277 in their fleet. *Fred Ivey*

TRAFFIC CIRCULAR FOR 19th MAY 1950

493 Routes, 657, 667—Operation from Hanwell Depot on Whit Monday

Notice to Inspectors and Conductors, Fulwell and Hanwell Depots.

On Whit Monday certain trolleybuses will operate from Hanwell Depot between Hammersmith and Hampton Court, and Shepherds Bush and Hampton Court.

1. **Fares and Tickets (Hanwell Depot):**

   A farebill for Route 667 will be exhibited in Hanwell Depot.

   When running between Half Acre, Brentford and Hanwell Depot, fares will be charged as on Route 655 and the present farestage point numbers will be used.

   When running between Hammersmith or Shepherds Bush and Hampton Court, farestage point numbers as shown on the route 667 farebill will be used. In order to conform to the practice on T.I. Machines used at Fulwell Depot, conductors will punch tickets in the farestage and point number at which the passenger boards the trolleybus.

2. **Route Nos.:**

   When leaving Hampton Court for Shepherds Bush—Show Route No. 657.

   When leaving Hampton Court for Hammersmith—Show Route No. 667.

   When running to Hampton Court—Show Route No. 667.

3. **Destinations Blinds (Hanwell Depot).**

   The following wording must be shown:

When Running to	Show Front and Rear		Side	
	No.	Wording	No.	Wording
Hampton Ct.	25	Hampton Court via Brentford & Twickenham		Chiswick Kew
Hammersmith	26	Hammersmith Broadway via Twickenham and Brentford	9	Brentford Twickenham Hampton
	27	via Twickenham and Brentford Shepherds Bush		

494 Route 628—Operation from Wandsworth Depot on Whit Monday

On Whit Monday a part of Route 628 will operate from Wandsworth Depot.
A specimen farebill will be exhibited in the depot.

Destination Blinds

The following wording must be shown:

When Running to	Show Front and Rear		Side
	No.	Wording	Wording
Craven Park	10	Craven Park via Harlesden	Wandsworth Putney Hammersmith Shepherds Bush Harlesden
Clapham Junction	8	Clapham Junction via Harlesden	
Depot	2	Wandsworth Station	

495 Ticket Boxes—Whitsun Arrangements

The following arrangements will apply to ticket boxes dispatched from Effra Road, covering the Whitsun Holiday period:

SOUTHERN DIVISION
Excluding Camberwell and Wandsworth Depots

Wednesday, 24th May Thursday, 25th May	Two Day Box—As normal
Friday, 26th May Saturday, 27th May Sunday, 28th May	Three Day Box
Monday, 29th May Tuesday, 30th May	Two Day Box—As normal

NORTHERN DIVISION
and Camberwell and Wandsworth Depots

Thursday, 25th May Friday, 26th May	Two Day Box—As normal
Saturday, 27th May Sunday, 28th May Monday, 29th May	Three Day Box
Tuesday, 30th May Wednesday, 31st May	Two Day Box—As normal

The normal schedule for delivery and collection of the ticket boxes will be maintained but boxes will not be specially labelled to indicate the three day working.

(o) <u>Hanwell Depot: Extension of overhead wiring from Nos. 1, 2 and 3 roads to Traverser Pit.</u> W. & B.E. Est. £25 - Elect. Engr's. Est. D.116. £60. Total cost £85.

Inconvenience and delay is caused by the necessity for moving on batteries all trolleybuses from the traverser to Nos. 1, 2 and 3 roads, and this will be obviated by extending the overhead wiring to the traverser. This work was contemplated prior to the war but was deferred when hostilities commenced.

APPROVED:

(q) <u>Hanwell Depot: Installation of Romesse stove.</u> W. & B.E. Est. B.4609. £22.
Staff have complained for a long time of the lack of heating in the Stores and it is proposed to install a Romesse stove.

APPROVED:

TRAFFIC CIRCULAR FOR 16th APRIL 1943

Route 660—   3180

OPERATION FROM HANWELL DEPOT

Commencing on Wednesday, 21st April, 1943, certain trolleybuses will operate between Craven Park and Hammersmith via Acton.

Fares

Fares will be charged as on Routes 660 and 666 and a revised farebill will be exhibited in the depot.

Tickets

Routes 660/666 tickets for the following values will be supplied in addition to route 607/655 tickets. 3d. and 4d. ordinary single, 2½d., 3d. and 4d. workman returns.

Destination Blinds

When running to	Show Front and Rear		Show Side		Number
	No.	Wording	No.	Wording	
Craven Park	—	Craven Park	—	Harlesden, Willesden Lane, Horn Lane, Acton, Starch Green	660
Hammersmith	—	Hammersmith Broadway	—		660

OPERATION FROM HAMMERSMITH DEPOT

Commencing on Wednesday, 21st April, 1943, certain trolleybuses will operate between Craven Park and Hammersmith via Acton.

Fares

Fares will be charged as on Routes 660 and 666 and a revised farebill will be exhibited in the depot.

When running to or from Hammermith Depot via Scrubs Lane, workman return tickets will not be issued for journeys overlapping both Acton Market Place and Scrubs Lane, Harrow Road.

Tickets

Route 660/666 tickets for the following values will be supplied in addition to Route 626/628/630 tickets. 3d. and 4d. ordinary single, 2½d., 3d., 4d. and 5d. workman returns.

Destination Blinds

When Running to	Show Front and Rear		Show Side		Number
	No.	Wording	No.	Wording	
Craven Park (from Acton)	3A	Craven Park	7	Jubilee Clock, Old Oak Lane, North Acton Station, Acton Station, Horn Lane	660
Hammersmith (from Acton)	3	Hammersmith Broadway	7		660
Acton (from Depot via Scrubs Lane)	9	Via Harlesden, Acton Market Place	2	Wandsworth, Putney, Hammersmith, Harlesden, Acton	626

STAFF TROLLEYBUS JOURNEYS

HANWELL Routes 607, 655

	Nights of Sun/Mon to Fri/Sat.							Night of Sat/Sun.						
	607	607	655	607	607	607	655	607	607	655	607	607	607	655
Uxbridge				1.32	3.27						1.32			
Hayes End				1.46	3.41						1.46	4.30		
Southall (Delamere Road)		12.14		1.55	3.50				12.14		1.55	4.39		
Hanwell Broadway		12.25	12.30	2. 6	4. 1		4.12		12.25	12.30	2. 6	4.50		5. 0
Brentford			12.41				4.24			12.41				5.11
Brentford			12.43				4.27			12.43				5.17
Hanwell Broadway	12. 1		12.54	12.56	2.50		4.39	12. 1		12.54	12.56	4. 7		5.28
Southall (Delamere Rd.)	12.12			1. 7	3. 1			12.12			1. 7	4.18		
Hayes End				1.16	3.10						1.16	4.27		
Uxbridge				1.30	3.24						1.30			

319

Blind 1 (left):

PRIVATE
TO HIRE A BUS OR COACH
APPLY: 55 BROADWAY S.W.1
ABBEY 5600

ACTON VALE
(BROMYARD AVE)
VIA HANWELL

ACTON
MARKET PLACE

SOUTHALL
DELAMERE RD
HAYES END RD
VIA HANWELL

SHEPHERDS BUSH
ACTON
HANWELL

UXBRIDGE
BRENTFORD
HALF ACRE
HANWELL
BROADWAY
CLAPHAM JUNCTION
BRENTFORD
HAMMERSMITH

ACTON VALE
BRENTFORD
HANWELL

HAMMERSMITH BDY
BRENTFORD
CHISWICK

HANWELL BDY
VIA HORN LANE

ACTON
MARKET PLACE
VIA BRENTFORD

KEW BRIDGE
VIA CHISWICK

Blind 2:

CHISWICK
YOUNGS CORNER

HAMMERSMITH
BROADWAY

FULHAM PALACE RD
EDGARLEY TERRACE

HILLINGDON CHURCH
AND
STRATFORD BDG

HAMPTON COURT
BRENTFORD
TWICKENHAM

HAMMERSMITH BDY
TWICKENHAM
BRENTFORD

SHEPHERDS BUSH
BRENTFORD
CHISWICK

HOUNSLOW

29.4.57

Despite route 655 not running via Horn Lane since 1937 it is still included in blinds made in 1960.

Youngs Corner and Stamford Brook Station are the same location.

The lazy display for Hillingdon Church is erroneous - there should not be the word AND; STRATFORD BDG should be the qualifying point. The panel indicates that there is a shuttle service between the top and bottom of Hillingdon Hill! It is possible that the blind compilers may have got misled by the West Ham panel illustrated below.

Blind 3:

PRIVATE
TO HIRE A BUS OR COACH
APPLY: 55 BROADWAY S.W.1
ABBEY 5600 OR ANY LOCAL OFFICE

ACTON VALE
(BROMYARD AVE)
VIA HANWELL

ACTON
MARKET PLACE

SOUTHALL
DELAMERE RD
HAYES END RD
VIA HANWELL

SHEPHERDS BUSH
ACTON
HANWELL

UXBRIDGE
BRENTFORD
HALF ACRE
HANWELL
BROADWAY
CLAPHAM JUNCTION
BRENTFORD
HAMMERSMITH

ACTON VALE
BRENTFORD
HANWELL

HAMMERSMITH BDY
BRENTFORD
CHISWICK

HANWELL BDY
VIA HORN LANE

ACTON
MARKET PLACE
VIA BRENTFORD

KEW BRIDGE
VIA CHISWICK

Blind 4:

STAMFORD BROOK
STATION

HAMMERSMITH
BROADWAY

FULHAM PALACE RD
EDGARLEY TERRACE

HILLINGDON CHURCH
AND
STRATFORD BDG

HAMPTON COURT
BRENTFORD
TWICKENHAM

HAMMERSMITH BDY
TWICKENHAM
BRENTFORD

SHEPHERDS BUSH
BRENTFORD
CHISWICK

HOUNSLOW

2.8.60

When this blind was produced it included 657/667 displays that had been last used the previous day. The PRIVATE panel is a Country Bus display. Hanwell vehicles never ran to Hounslow.

Panel:

EAST HAM TOWN HALL
AND
STRATFORD BDY

25.2.52

EXTRA
607
655
667
657

29.4.58

21.6.49

607
SHEPHERDS BUSH
ACTON
HANWELL
SOUTHALL
HAYES
607

655
HANWELL
BRENTFORD

HAMMERSMITH
655
HANWELL
BRENTFORD
HAMMERSMITH
WANDSWORTH
667
CHISWICK
KEW
BRENTFORD
TWICKENHAM
HAMPTON
667

657
CHISWICK
KEW
BUSCH CORNER
ISLEWORTH
HOUNSLOW
657

607
SHEPHERDS BUSH
ACTON
HANWELL
SOUTHALL
HAYES
607

655
HANWELL
BRENTFORD
HAMMERSMITH
655
HANWELL
BRENTFORD
HAMMERSMITH
WANDSWORTH
667
CHISWICK
KEW
BRENTFORD
TWICKENHAM
HAMPTON
667

657
CHISWICK
KEW
BUSCH CORNER
ISLEWORTH
HOUNSLOW
657

4.1.60

Despite Acton closing to trolleybuses in 1937, blinds produced for Hanwell after that were dated in this manner.

On the side blinds the gaps between BRENTFORD and HAMMERSMITH on the 655 are deliberate for, by careful positioning, respective short workings to these two points are accommodated. Two displays are included for the 667 despite Hanwell only working journeys the full length of the route. Hanwell did not operate the proper 657 service; despite this, full details are given - even a short-working display.

ACTON

Opened 5th April 1936, this depot was a 'stop gap' facility until building work was completed at Hanwell and Stonebridge. Minimal alterations were made to the building - little more than adding a positive running wire.

Closed to trolleybuses on 9th March 1937. Used as a tower wagon base until 1962.
Routes operated 607, 655, 660, 666.
Type used: AEC and Leyland.
Capacity: Not known.
Last trolleybus into depot: Not known.

A2 52 is in Acton depot on 21st January 1932; delivered the previous September it will have not run many miles. One trolley boom is on the positive tram overhead; a wire leads from the back of 52 onto a tram rail giving a return electrical negative contact that enables the trolleybus to be powered. Components are set out as training aids on adjacent benches; these allow electricians to understand the workings of a trolleybus, hence the presence of 52 which has an AEC badge on the dummy radiator and a BTH one under the canopy.
London Transport Museum U10358

277 was licensed on 12th August 1936 and available for service at Stonebridge Park depot on 23rd August. This view is likely to have been taken between these two dates and during the short period of dual tram and trolleybus operation here - 5th April to 14th November 1936. Number 277 was one of three C2s that were operational until 10th November 1959. EXTRA and PRIVATE were the first displays on front and rear destination and route blinds at this time. On the left are a couple of ancient LUT cars - the one on the right is T class tram 2352 (formerly LUT 336) which is ready to go out on route 55.
J.W. Stuchlik

Acton was the fourth depot to operate trolleybuses – but did so for just under a year. First vehicle out (at about 8.40am) on Sunday 5th April 1936 was C2 186 on route 660 which will take on passengers in the High Street in a couple of minutes time. A number of officials attend to ensure that everything goes to plan. For the next three months staff will work only between Acton and Hammersmith; very mundane for them. It will not be until 5th July that crews spread their wings – this is when the 660 is temporarily withdrawn and replaced by route 666, which will operate between Edgware and Hammersmith. There may only be one number and two destination displays on the blinds; Acton was the first depot to use the revised style of route numbers. The second 660 due out is immediately behind.

C2 184 and D2 461 are at the entrance to the depot on 20th January 1937. Having been allocated some C class vehicles when they worked on routes 660/666 and then some D2s when they operated on the 607/655 there was a period when AECs and Leylands worked here simultaneously; the short-lived ACTON DEPOT display is shown on both vehicles. Overhead only allows vehicles to enter and leave eastwards; the loose-leaf diagram shows an unfulfilled proposal for connections to and from the west. Ekins of Hertford were responsible for work modifying the tram depot in 1936 for short term trolleybus operation; their sign has been left up for business opportunities. Acorn sub-station was an integral part of Acton depot.

London Transport Museum U22707

Taken at the same time as the previous photo, 461 has its side and interior lights on, and is being prepared for service. Signs inform staff that the maximum speed in the depot is 4 mph and that smoking is strictly prohibited. The Hillman car BXD 521, is allocated to the tram and trolleybus department; is a London Transport bigwig checking up on matters? The LPTB had a number of vehicles with this marque; BXD 520 was STL 850. Near the top of the building the year of the depot's construction (1895) is displayed on the brickwork.

London Transport Museum U22705

OFFICE OF THE ROLLING STOCK ENGINEER,
(ROAD SERVICES),
CHISWICK.

J. SCHOFIELD, ESQ.,
WORKS ENGINEER,
CHARLTON.

C16/4/D.907

12th March, 1951.

TROLLEYBUSES - PERMANENT ALLOCATION

I append copy of the permanent allocation of trolleybuses as at 6th March, 1951.

DEPOT	TOTAL LICENSED	LICENSED TROLLEYBUSES AT DEPOT
Bow	105	1549-1564, 1566-1570, 1572-1586, 1588-1656
Edmonton	129	803A, 861A, 891-904, 1069-1097, 1155-1198, 1230-1238, 1278, 1280, 1281, 1315, 1318, 1329, 1672-1694, 1696, 1697.
Ilford	41	1722-1735, 1737, 1738, 1740-1764
Poplar	90	1430-1491, 1493-1520.
Stam. Hill	71	1098-1122, 1123A, 1124-1127, 1128A, 1129-1137, 1199-1229
Walthamstow	103	303, 305-307, 324, 325, 329, 330, 333-347, 349-353, 355, 358, 360, 362, 366, 367, 369, 370, 372, 374-376, 379, 380, 382, 383, 420-422, 450, 457, 478, 479, 481, 482, 502-519, 555, 556, 561, 564, 569, 967, 969-982, 1270-1277, 1279, 1282-1284.
Westham	157	95A, 107A, 406A, 477, 565, 566, 568, 570-574, 575C, 576, 578C, 579-581, 585, 587-590, 592, 594-598, 600, 601, 602C, 603-620, 621A, 622, 623C, 624, 625, 626C, 627, 628, 630-632, 633C, 634, 635C, 636, 637, 639, 640, 641C, 642, 643C, 644-649, 651, 1381-1384, 1385B, 1386, 1388-1406, 1521-1542, 1544, 1546-1548, 1657-1670, 1698, 1699, 1704, 1711-1719, 1721, 653.
Clapton	79	1138-1149, 1151-1154, 1239-1243, 1244A, 1245, 1246, 1248-1269, 1285A, 1286-1314, 1321-1323.
Lea Bridge	28	1324-1327, 1331-1354.
N.E. Division	803	
Bexley	86	94, 96, 97C, 98, 104, 106, 385C, 388, 389C, 390B, 391B, 392B, 393, 395B, 396C, 397C, 399, 400, 401, 402C, 403, 404, 405B, 407B, 408, 409B, 410, 411, 412B, 413, 414, 415C, 416, 419C, 423-427, 429, 431, 434, 439-442, 444, 451B, 468, 469, 470B, 471-476, 480, 483, 765, 766B, 784B, 785, 786B, 788, 789, 790B, 793, 794B, 796-798, 799B, 800, 801B, 802, 804B, 805-807, 808B, 809-811, 813, 850.
SE Division	86	
Carshalton	33	489-491, 493, 64-75, 77-93.
Fulwell	92	160-173, 1565A, 1587A, 1765-1817, 1819-1841.
H'smith	75	433, 436-438, 443, 445-447, 449, 452-466, 496-501, 520-553, 1700-1703, 1705-1710, 1720.
Isleworth	30	61, 63, 132-159
S.W. Division	230	

Note that the typist has misspelt West Ham.

P.T.O.

DEPOT	TOTAL LICENSED	LICENSED TROLLEYBUSES AT DEPOT
Colindale	41	201-232,235,238-241,293-295,300.
Finchley	81	301,302,308-316,318-323,326,328,331,332,754,905-952,955-963, 965,966
Hanwell	115	654-753,1055-1068,384
Highgate	168	62,100-103,105,108-131,484-488,492,494,495,954,983-992, 993B,994-1000,1001B,1002-1006,1007B,1008-1054,1247A,1316, 1317,1319,1320,1328,1330,1355-1378,1380,1407-1429,1543B, 1545B.
Stone.Park	100	174-200,233,234,236,237,242-292,296-299,304,348,354,356,357, 359,361,363,365,371,377,381,368,378.
Wood Green	104	755-764,767-783,792A,795A,814-849,851-860,862-890.
N.W.Division	609	

Trolleybus 378 Stonebridge Park, is licensed for training only.

UNLICENSED TROLLEYBUSES

Finchley Depot	11,13,19,32,33,37,48,54. Fulwell Depot.7. West Ham Depot,58
Hanwell Depot	1671.
Fulwell Works	76,430,1818.
Chiswick Tram Depot	554,557,558,559,560,562,563,567,577,582,583,584,586,591, 593,599.
Charlton & West Ham Works	317,327,373,417,432,629,638,650,652,964,968,1150,1571,1695, 1736,1739.

Licensed Trolleybuses 1728
Unlicensed " 46
TOTAL 1,774

COPIES TO:
T.T. Shephard, Esq., V.C. Wormald, Esq., Mr. Faulkner, Dunlop Tyre Co. Mr. Lane Charlton Works, Mr. Girling, Fulwell Works (2), Mr. Jolley Fulwell Works, Mr. Creed, Mr. Shurey, Divisional Engineers, N.E., N.W., S.W., S.E. and Mr. Ayliffe (2)

ROLLING STOCK ENGINEER (ROAD SERVICES)

Office of the
ROLLING STOCK ENGINEER,
(ROAD SERVICES),
CHISWICK.

C16/4/D.313.

To: J. SCHOFIELD, ESQ.,
WORKS MANAGER (TRAMS & TROLLEYBUSES),
CHARLTON WORKS.

16th August, 1951.

TROLLEYBUSES - PERMANENT ALLOCATION

I append copy of the permanent allocation of trolleybuses as at 14th August, 1951.

DEPOT	TOTAL LICS'D.	LICENSED TROLLEYBUSES AT DEPOT
Bow	105	1549-1564, 1566-1573, 1575-1586, 1588-1656.
Edmonton	130	803A, 861A, 891-904, 1069-1097, 1155-1198, 1230-1238, 1278, 1280, 1281, 1315, 1318, 1329, 1672-1697.
Ilford	41	1722-1737, 1739-1745, 1747-1764.
Poplar	90	1430-1491, 1493-1520.
Stamford Hill	70	1068-1117, 1119-1122, 1123A, 1124-1127, 1128A, 1129-1137, 1199-1229.
Walthamstow	108	305-307, 324, 325, 329, 330, 333-337, 339-347, 349-353, 355, 358, 360, 362, 366, 367, 369, 372-376, 379, 380, 382, 383, 420-422, 467, 477-479, 481, 482, 502-519, 554, 556-564, 569, 967-982, 1270-1277, 1279, 1282-1284.
West Ham	157	95A, 107A, 406A, 565-568, 570, 574, 575C, 576, 578C, 580, 582-584, 586, 588, 589, 591, 593-601, 602C, 604-620, 621A, 622, 623A, 624, 625, 626C, 627, 628, 630-632, 633C, 634, 635C, 636-640, 641C, 642, 643C, 644-653, 1381, 1382, 1384, 1385B, 1386, 1389-1406, 1521-1542, 1544, 1546-1548, 1657-1670, 1698, 1699, 1704, 1711-1719, 1721, 629C, 577.
Clapton	78	1138-1154, 1239-1243, 1244A, 1245, 1246, 1248, 1250-1269, 1285A, 1286-1313, 1321-1323.
Lea Bridge	28	1324-1327, 1331-1354.
	807	N.E. DIVISION TOTAL
Bexley	83	94, 96, 97C, 98C, 104, 106, 385C, 388, 389C, 390B, 391B, 392B, 393, 395B, 396C, 397C, 399, 400, 401, 402C, 403, 404, 405B, 407B, 408, 409B, 410, 412B, 414, 415C, 419C, 416, 417, 423, 424, 426, 427, 429-432, 439-442, 444, 451B, 468, 469, 470B, 471-476, 480, 483, 765, 784B, 785, 786B, 789, 790B, 793, 794B, 796-798, 799B, 800, 802, 801B, 805-807, 808B, 809-811, 813, 850, 788.
	83	S.E. DIVISION TOTAL

P.T.O.

DEPOT	TOTAL LICS'D.	LICENSED TROLLEYBUSES AT DEPOTS
Carshalton	32	64-72, 75-93, 489-491, 493.
Fulwell	94	61, 160-173, 1565A, 1587A, 1765-1841.
Hammersmith	75	433, 436-438, 443, 445-447, 449, 452-466, 496-501, 520-553, 1700-1703, 1705-1710, 1720.
Isleworth	30	63, 132-159, 376.
	231	S.W. DIVISION TOTAL
Colindale	41	201-232, 235, 238-241, 293-295, 300.
Finchley	81	301, 302, 308-323, 326-328, 331, 754, 905-952, 955-958, 960, 961, 963-966.
Hanwell	116	304, 654-753, 1055-1068, 1671.
Highgate	167	62, 100-103, 105, 108-115, 117-131, 484-488, 492, 494, 495, 954, 983-992, 993B, 994-1000, 1001B, 1002-1006, 1007B, 1008-1054, 1247A, 1316, 1317, 1319, 1320, 1328, 1330, 1355-1364, 1366-1380, 1407-1429, 1543B, 1545B.
Stonebridge Pk.	99	174-200, 233, 234, 236, 237, 242-292, 296-299, 304, 348, 354, 356, 357, 359, 361, 363, 365, 371, 377, 381, 368.
Wood Green	104	755-764, 767-783, 792A, 795A, 814-849, 851-860, 862-890.
	608	N.W. DIVISION TOTAL

Trolleybus 61 is licensed for training only.

DELICENSED TROLLEYBUSES

Finchley	11, 13, 19, 32, 33, 37, 48, 54, 58 (Waiting disposal)
Fulwell	7 (Waiting disposal)
Fulwell Works	73, 74.
Highgate	116
Charlton & West Ham	303, 332, 338, 370, 411, 413, 425, 434, 450, 766B, 804B, 959, 962, 1118, 1249, 1314, 1383, 1388, 1574, 1738, 1746.
Chiswick Tram Depot	555, 571, 572, 573, 579, 581, 585, 587, 590, 592, 603.

```
Licensed trolleybuses   1729
Delicensed     "          45
         Total         1774
```

ROLLING STOCK ENGINEER
(ROAD SERVICES)

Copies to: T.T. Shephard, Esq., V.C. Wormald, Esq.,

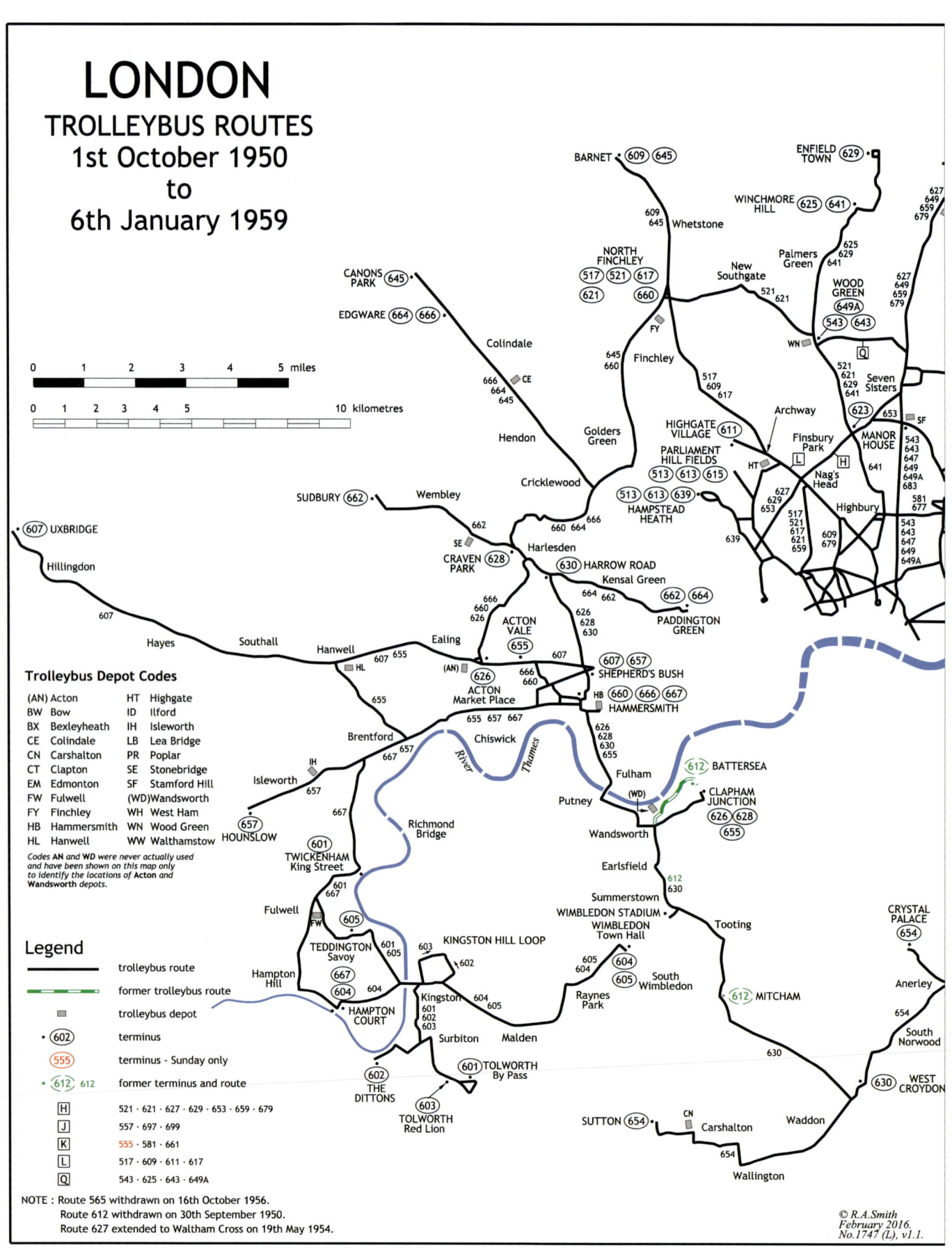

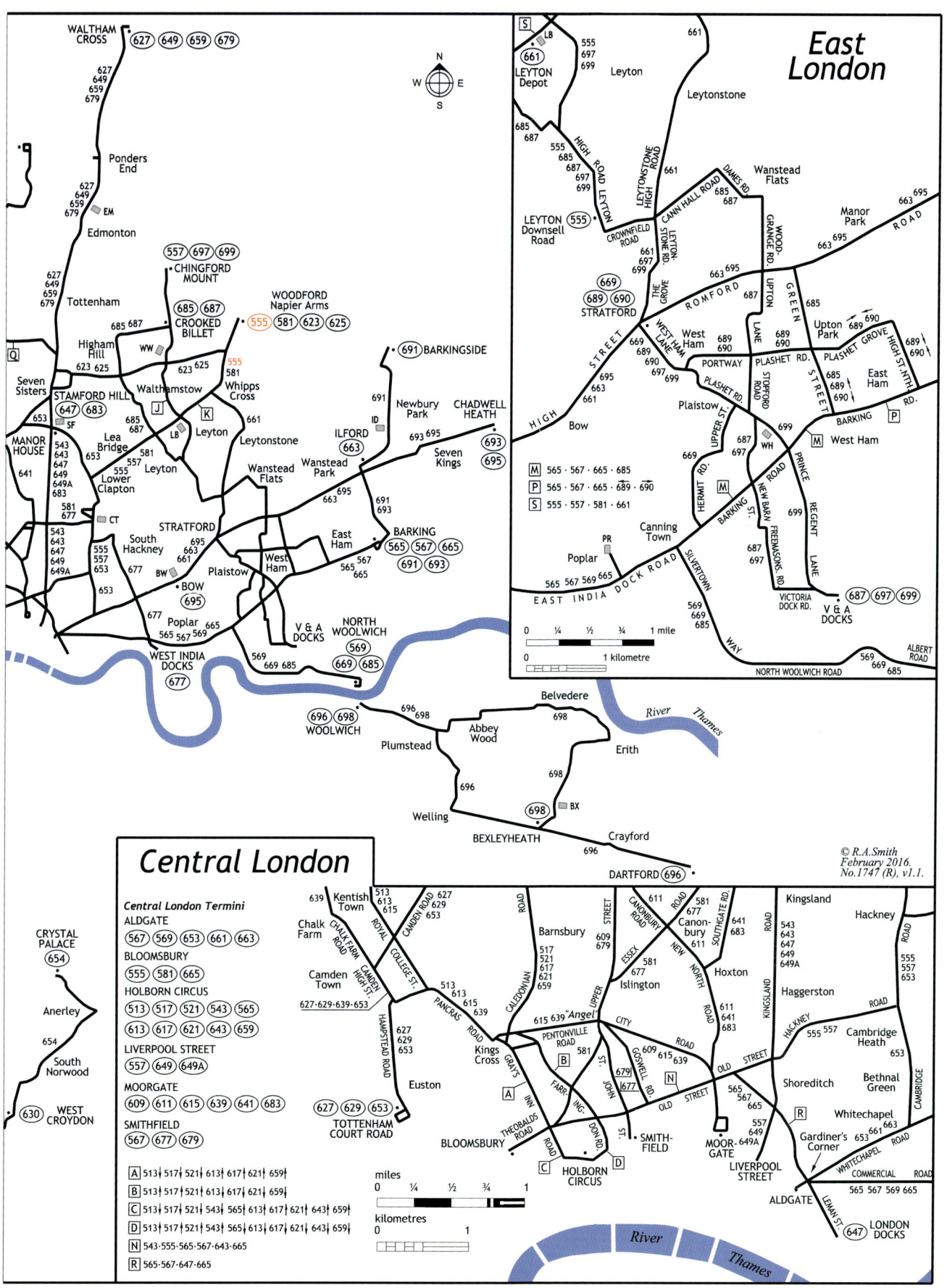

A TROLLEYBUS CONDUCTRESS AT NINETEEN

My father, Charles Sullivan, was trolleybus conductor T9029 at Bexleyheath depot; he took me to work sometimes and allowed me to take tickets out of his rack, put them in the punch and ping it and then give them to passengers who'd paid a fare. I rode for free and sat downstairs. I liked seeing him doing his job. He had to get out at some places to pull a handle that made the trolleybus go one way or the other. Sometimes he pulled out a long pole out from under the trolleybus – it made a rumbling noise coming out and going back. I thought he was very strong moving those poles. Whoever would have thought I would be a 'frog puller' and 'trolley boom mover' in years to come. Everybody at the depot knew me because when I was a young girl I used to help my dad with his waybill in the conductors' room; as I grew up I was never a stranger there and it was like one big family. From when I was about fourteen I became very interested in this handsome conductor called Raymond Cole (of which more anon).

London Transport had a chronic shortage of staff in the mid-nineteen fifties; I'd always wanted to be a conductress so decided to follow in dad's footsteps. In mid-1957, when nineteen, I went to Griffith House to apply for this work. I thought I'd be accepted straightaway because of the staff shortage; they turned me down on the basis of age. Undeterred, dad spoke to the Union rep at the depot; even though it was legal to employ eighteen year olds, London Transport weren't keen on it. However, it was agreed by the powers-that-be and I joined up while still a teenager. I had a medical and passed the arithmetic test and was told I would work at Bexleyheath trolleybus depot; this was the location I wanted to work at. I applied for a **LICENCE TO ACT AS CONDUCTOR OF TROLLEY VEHICLES.**

This is me - Jean. I am wearing my London Transport jacket.
Jean Cole

Dad took me to Chiswick where I collected my uniform and was given a staff pass; I had to go to Manor House divisional office for three days classroom training. I went by bus and Underground; it was a very long day given the distance involved. Training was with the Gibson ticket machine; however, there was a girl who was going to West Ham which still used the ticket and punch system. Because she was training on it we also had to have a go with it; when a Gibson failed I put a pencil hole through emergency punch tickets that were kept in the conductors' box. *Jean has excellent recall as Poplar and West Ham were the last locations on the London Transport network to use the punch and ticket system – 4th October 1958.*

I had been to north London before to see relatives; dad had taken me by "trolley" to Woolwich where we got a tram to Westminster. Whenever he got on a tram though, he fell asleep!

Gibson Ticket Machines 182
Method of Ticket Issue

Cases where Gibson Ticket Machines have become jammed have frequently been caused by the previous ticket having been torn off incorrectly, resulting in the paper becoming rucked inside the ticket roll cover. In order to avoid this trouble, conductors are reminded that tickets should be torn off with an **upward and sideways movement.**

TICKET ISSUING MACHINES

The method of indicating the class of ticket issued to passengers is clearly defined in the instructions on the operation of ticket machines.

It is important that all tickets are correctly classified especially tickets for child fares when the Code Letter "C" must be used.

What happens if a conductress loses a machine in her charge?!

Private—NOT for Publication

TRAFFIC CIRCULAR No. 17
CENTRAL ROAD SERVICES

To operate on and from Friday, 17th August, 1956, unless otherwise stated.

GIBSON TICKET MACHINES

It is the responsibility of staff to take proper care of equipment issued to them to ensure against loss or damage whilst in their charge.

The Ticket Machine is a costly item of equipment and it is therefore important and in their own interest that Conductors should take special care of the machine whilst it is in their charge. Conductors should retain it in their possession at all times on duty and especially during meal relief or lay-over periods at terminal points.

If a ticket machine is lost or damaged whilst in his charge the Conductor may, at the discretion of the Executive, be held responsible for the cost of replacement or repair of the machine.

61

The conductress of number 444 looks towards the back of the vehicle as people board. As soon as the platform is clear she'll ring the bell cord a couple of times so that her driver knows it is safe to go. The driver looks in his mirror which shows the platform. We were supposed to ring the 'bus off from the platform but often we did it in the manner my colleague does here. She is wearing her thick winter uniform overcoat on 2nd March 1959.
Alan Cross

FARES
ROUTE 696—WOOLWICH & DARTFORD (F.T.365) (Dec. 1955)
via Welling

Stage Point No.													
	1												Woolwich, Parsons Hill–1
	2	2½											Beresford Square–2†
	3	2½	2½										Plumstead Station–3
	4	4	2½	2½									Wickham Lane, Plumstead Corner–4
	5	4	4	2½	2½								Plumstead L.T. Garage–5
	6	6	4	4	2½	2½							Wickham Lane, Foresters Arms–6
	7	6	6	4	4	2½	2½						Lovel Avenue–7
	8	8	6	6	4	4	2½	2½					Welling Corner–8
	9	8	8	6	6	4	4	2½	2½				Danson Road or Brampton Road–9
	10	10	8	8	6	6	4	4	2½	2½			Lion Road–10
2½	15	10	8	8	8	6	6	4	4	2½	2½		Bexleyheath Market Place–15
2½	16	1/-	10	8	8	6	6	4	4	2½	2½		Pinnacle Hill–16
4	17	1/-	10	10	8	8	6	6	4	4	2½	2½	Old Road, Gas Works Corner–17
4	18	1/2	1/-	10	10	8	8	6	6	4	4	2½	2½	Crayford Bridge or Station Road–18
6	19	1/2	1/-	1/-	10	10	8	8	6	6	4	4	2½	2½	Princes Road North–19
6	20	1/4	1/2	1/2	1/-	1/-	10	8	8	6	6	4	4	2½	2½	Havelock Road P.O.–20
8	21	1/4	1/2	1/2	1/2	1/-	1/-	10	10	8	8	6	6	4	4	2½	2½	Tower Road–21
8	22	1/4	1/2	1/2	1/2	1/2	1/-	1/-	10	10	8	8	6	6	4	4	2½	2½	Dartford, Market Street–22

Left column (Bexleyheath L.T. Depot–14): 2½, 2½, 4, 4, 6, 6, 8, 8

† – Farezone

14	—	—	—	—	—	—	4	4	2½	2½	Barnehurst Bridge–14
13	—	—	—	—	—	6	4	4	2½	2½	Brook Street–13
12	—	—	—	—	—	6	6	4	4	2½	2½	Carlton Road–12
11	—	—	—	—	—	8	6	6	4	4	2½	2½	Erith, Wheatley Arms–11

14	1/-	10	10	8	8	6	6	4	4	2½	2½	Bexleyheath L.T. Depot–14

EARLY MORNING SINGLE FARES

Where the Ordinary Single fare is	Early Morning Single fare will be
8d. – 1/4	7d.

Ticket Issuing Machines— Paper Roll Cores 139
Conductors using Ticket Machines are again reminded that Ticket Roll Cores must be placed in the ticket machine container and handed in on completion of duty and not discarded on the bus or in the roadway.

Position of Conductors on Vehicles 140
Except when engaged upon the collection of fares, answering inquiries and the performance of other such duties, conductors should be on the platform of their vehicles, ready to attend to passengers and on the alert for intending passengers.

FARES
ROUTE 698—WOOLWICH & BEXLEYHEATH (R)
via Erith

Stage Point No.												
1												Woolwich, Parsons Hill or Market Hill–1
2	2											Beresford Square–2
3	2	2										Perrott Street–3
4	2	2	2									Plumstead Station–4
5	3	2	2	2								Lakedale Road–5
6	3	3	2	2	2							Wickham Lane, Plumstead Corner–6
7	5	3	3	2	2	2						Bostall Lane–7
8	5	5	3	3	3	2	2					Harrow Manorway, Abbey Wood–8
9	6	5	5	5	3	3	2	2				Railway Farm–9
10	6	6	5	5	5	3	2	2	2			Belvedere Station–10
11	8	6	6	6	5	5	3	3	2	2		Mayfield Road–11
12	8	8	6	6	6	5	3	3	3	2	2	Maxim Road–12
13	9	8	8	8	6	6	5	5	3	3	2	2	Wheatley Arms, Erith–13
14	9	9	8	8	8	6	5	5	3	3	2	2	Carlton Road–14
15	11	9	9	9	8	8	6	6	5	5	3	3	2	2	Brook Street–15
16	11	11	9	9	9	8	6	6	5	5	3	3	2	2	Barnehurst Bridge–16
17	1/0	11	11	11	9	9	8	8	6	6	5	5	3	3	2	2	Bexleyheath, Market Place–17

WHEN WORKING

18					8	8	6	6	5	5	3	3	2	2	Pinnacle Hill–18
19					9	8	8	6	6	5	5	3	3	2	2	Old Road, Gas Works Corner–19
20					9	9	8	8	6	6	5	5	3	3	2	2	Crayford Bridge or Station Road–20
21					11	9	9	8	8	6	6	5	5	3	3	2	2	Princes Road–21
22					11	11	9	9	8	8	6	6	5	5	3	3	2	2	Havelock Road, Post Office–22
23					1/0	11	11	9	9	8	8	6	6	5	5	3	3	2	2	Tower Road–23
24					1/0	1/0	11	11	9	9	8	8	6	6	5	5	3	3	2	2	Dartford, Market Street–24

I had to report to the depot one Thursday morning; later in the day I did part of a shift with a conductor-instructor; after that I was with different instructors on varying duties for five days. Fare collecting, money taking, frog pulling, buying teas, calling out stops and so on. I was told I had to change all blinds except the front destinations on any trolleybus that had an A, B or C after its fleet number and those numbered above 789; I soon knew which ones had the front destination blind changed by the driver. Of course everybody at the depot knew I was Charles' daughter and there was not much that the conductor-instructors could teach me that I didn't know already. I quickly learned the order of the blind displays and where frog handles needed pulling. Then back to Chiswick for two days where I was issued with badge T 20786 - a brand new one.

First day by myself was a Saturday late turn. There were many duties 'cut' because of staff shortage and I rolled off over 1,000 tickets. At the end of my first spell of duty my hands were filthy with all the coins I'd taken. When I finished the shift I said to myself 'I'm not going in tomorrow'. I did though and it was okay as it was a Sunday and quieter in terms of the numbers of passengers carried. Soon I was on the rota and would do all the duties in turn. If my dad or I wanted a change of duty or rest day we did it between ourselves - we had to sign a form and submit it a day beforehand.

> Private—NOT for Publication.
>
> **TRAFFIC CIRCULAR** No. 19
> CENTRAL ROAD SERVICES
>
> To operate on and from Friday, 14th September, 1956, unless otherwise stated.
>
> ### DESTINATION INDICATORS
>
> In the interest of efficient operation it is essential that destination indicators show correctly the route and destination of the vehicle. Conductors should alter and check the blinds of their vehicle at terminals and other specified points to ensure that correct sections are exposed for the next journey to be operated.
>
> Drivers should similarly alter and check the blinds under their control, either under the direction of the conductor or by means of the periscope where fitted.
>
> Destination indicators must be set to exhibit "Private" in the event of a breakdown or on any occasion when the vehicle is not operating on normal service.
>
> 71

> In no circumstances must Conductors turn the side indicator blinds upon trolleybuses, if the blinds are operated from the platform, while the trolleybus is in motion.

409B is on the 698 terminal loop at Bexleyheath Market Place; there was room for four trolleybuses to be on the stand together. A bamboo pole is hooked on the traction pole on the right – these were handy as they saved me bending down to drag out the bamboo from beneath the vehicle. This was a rebodied trolleybus and I had to remember not to change the side blind when the vehicle was moving. This was to avoid conductors coming coming into contact with parked vehicles - maybe there had been an incident in past times.

Despite there being some likelihood of trolleybuses arriving out of order at Parsons Hill, no loop was ever provided; this meant that occasionally one crew had to drop their poles to get past. 766B on the 698 by-passes 419C on the 696.
Fred Ivey

There were lots of 'shorts' to Abbey Wood; on route 698 on 2nd March 1959 number 399 has turned at the circle to wait on the siding until it is time to go. There was a lot of overhead here so drivers were particularly cautious going through it.
Alan Cross

It was a difficult turn at Princes Road; traffic zoomed up and down Crayford Road and we would have to wait for a gap to make the manoeuvre. Here, the driver is being extra vigilant and has opened his cab door to get a good view of Princes Road so as to line the trolleybus up perfectly. 471 is on the 696; in the background are five other trolleybuses, some of which will carry or have carried out the same exercise. *Fred Ivey*

Crayford reverser was where Crayford Road met Dartford Road; this view shows the difficulty of making the turn into Princes Road – as soon as 784B on the 696 is in Princes Road, two vehicles get on their way. In a few minutes time 784B will pick up workers from Vickers Car Factory. In this photograph, and the one above, the amplification to Crayford wrongly shows Princess Road instead of Princes Road. *Fred Ivey*

When Raymond was twenty-five he went on a trolleybus driving course. He passed his test and got badge number T8921 which was a re-issue. I found myself paired up with him from time to time. Heaven! In due course romance blossomed and I ended up marrying him, becoming Jean Cole. If it hadn't been for the 696 and 698 trolleybuses I wouldn't have married Raymond – and I am so very glad I did. A lot of courting and marrying went on with London Transport bus and trolleybus staff!

I soon settled into a life on trolleybuses and it was obvious that Bexleyheath Market Place was the hub of operations. There were two routes: 696 from Dartford to Woolwich, Parsons Hill via Welling and 698 from Bexleyheath to Woolwich via Erith; most turns did a bit on each route. However, there were some shifts that did five 'rounders' on the 698 and others that did three 'rounders' on the 696. Trolleybuses operated in a different manner to buses so there was a lot of interworking with the two routes. Essentially the two services were a 'system' within the London Transport trolleybus system. In the Monday to Friday afternoon peaks, five trolleybuses left the depot in quick succession for Crayford; between them they hardly picked up a soul. At Crayford we turned on a reversing triangle at Princes Road where there was always an inspector on duty; the 'buses might not have left the depot in order but the inspector ensured they all did so on departure. Conductors waved their drivers back as the manoeuvre was across a main road; it was alright in daylight but in the dark it was not safe. There was little illumination on a main road with trolleybuses reversing one after the other – five in five minutes. Setting off in the proper order we picked up workers from Vickers munitions factory with the 'buses – some showing 696, others 698 - going to different places. One went to Plumstead where it had to do another reverse; another came back to Crayford to reverse yet again. There was a facility on the fare chart to go from Dartford to Abbey Wood but if anyone wanted

There are a couple of interesting features in this view of 799B on route 698 proceeding through Beresford Square on its way to Parsons Hill. On the left is one of the entrances to Woolwich Arsenal; in the roadway are covered-over tram lines. A policeman directs traffic; however only a trolleybus and a car are benefiting from his services.
Fred Ivey

Now and again it was necessary to use the old loop at Woolwich Ferry; in the top left hand corner is the facing frog leading into the circle. Just about to pass under the overhead junction is 404 which has just started its long trip to Dartford on route 696. Note the tram track, last used in the very early hours of 6th July 1952, is still in place.
John Clarke

Approved Refreshment Places.

601	Twickenham Terminus.
602	Mrs. Rawlins General Stores, Portsmouth Road, The Dittons. (Order refreshments on northbound journeys and collect on southbound journeys.)
603	Tolworth Terminus.
604, 667	L.T.E. Canteen, Hampton Court.
605	Teddington Terminus.
607	Frank's Cafe, 354 Uxbridge Road, Southall.
612	306 York Road, Wandsworth. 184 Garratt Lane, Earlsfield.
626, 628, 655	2 Grant Road, Clapham Junction.
630	184 Garratt Lane, Earlsfield.
654	Betty's Cafe, 118 Anerley Road, Anerley.
657	Hownslow Terminus.
696	Hut Cafe, Upper Wickham Lane, East Wickham.
698	Elite Cafe, Church Street, Erith. *Sunday mornings before above Cafe is open—* Till's Cafe, 131B High Street, Plumstead.

* To be used on down journeys only, a.m.
To be used on up journeys only, p.m.

Note the misspelling of Hounslow.

I must have conducted a trolleybus to Dartford hundreds of times; one was 796 which is on the 696 stand at Market Street waiting to take a trip to Woolwich on 22nd August 1953. The blind shows WOOLWICH FERRY; the blind makers are out of sorts as the terminus had been at Parsons Hill for many years.
Peter Mitchell 0193

Despite there being a five minute headway on Saturday afternoons on route 698, the volume of shoppers was too much for the ordinary service and it had to be boosted whenever possible. The depot inspectors would get hold of some of us to do a bit of overtime. In this instance 793 backs up the service to Erith. EXTRA was always displayed at these times; I don't know whether it was protocol or whether London Transport wanted to show they were making the effort to help everyone out.

Fred Ivey

The one and only turn of the day to Villacourt Road on the 696 was at about half past seven in the morning on Mondays to Fridays. The photographer worked out that it would be best to see this trip as near as possible to conversion day to guarantee the light; this was achieved on 2nd March 1959 when 410 was photographed. Not only is Villacourt Road shown on the blind but also on the street sign above the shop. 410 has a dent on the front panel; the coachmakers are not going to do any panel beating this close to the conversion. *Alan Cross*

to go beyond Abbey Wood I had to work out the extra money or re-book them later on. There were some trips that went from Woolwich to Dartford via the 698 and the same fare thingy applied. Drivers didn't always get it right at Crayford reverser or the Plumstead one in Griffin Road; they went too far back and the poles came off. They had to go forwards on batteries to get back onto the overhead. Bamboo pole work here for Jean!

Back to Crayford. Although on 696 wires some were 698s with one going to Plumstead, another to Abbey Wood with one only going to Erith where it picked up more workers at the Fraser and Charmer factory. One day, having turned at Erith to pick them up, there was a power failure in the vicinity. The engineers told us we would have to push the 'bus past a certain number pole; everybody got off and myself and the passengers pushed it to a place where the electric was on. We all had quite a laugh because they had all paid their fares but had to walk quite a long way. With the end of the trolleys these 'odd' workings finished and those who used them had to transfer from 96 bus to 229 at Bexleyheath. When workers at Woolwich Arsenal turned out there were thousands who poured out of

Ladies dealing with trolley arms was historical at Bexleyheath as this view taken in the early part of the war shows. The date is deduced by the fact that this is number 792; its body was destroyed in a bomb attack on the depot on 7th November 1940. It was given a new body but never returned to Bexleyheath depot. The original position of a bullseye transfer on the rear of each vehicle was on the lower panel; a few years later it was decided to place it on the rear platform window. 792 has a bullseye in both positions; the lower one has yet to be removed. Whether it was erased before the body was destroyed is highly unlikely.

The lady is not amused and par for the course she is out the back of 396C which has dewired at Plumstead Corner on the final Saturday of operation (28th February 1959). Plumstead High Street meets Wickham Lane here where the 696 and 698 part company. There was a semi-electric frog here – something has gone wrong and 396C will require the services of a bamboo pole before it can get on its way to Bexleyheath on the 696.

John Gillham

Damage to Property Caused by Dewirements 54

Staff are reminded that

In every instance where damage is done to property by dewired trolleys the crew must report details on an "Accident Report Form."

One of the trolleybuses towed over from Fulwell was 496 which used to be at Hammersmith depot. The front advertisements are very clean for a vehicle that has been out of service for a few months. It is unlikely that new ones were put on during its stay with us so maybe it was kept under cover at Fulwell. 496 is in Watling Street Bexleyheath, heading east on the 696.
Fred Ivey

There were always some dumped vehicles at the back of the depot; 107A will not carry any more passengers. It was out of service for many months and was taken to Colindale depot a few days before we changed over to buses.
Peter Moore

the gates. I had to make sure I counted how many people could get on because they pushed and shoved so much I could be overpowered. For a time when the road was blocked at Parsons Hill all 696s/698s turned at the original terminus at the Free Ferry at Market Hill. Buses on route 75 also turned here so it could be a real squeeze to get everybody in. Some 696s/698s had to stay out on the main road until it was clear.

The 696 was the busier of the two routes, particularly as it was quicker to get from Woolwich to Bexleyheath. Sometimes we worked EXTRAS which was overtime; this was for activities at Danson Park so we would work Dartford to Welling Corner. When meetings took place in the evenings for Crayford Dogs we ran between Welling and Crayford beforehand; later on other crews picked the punters up and took them whence they had come. The 698 was extremely busy with shoppers on Saturday afternoons, Bexleyheath Market being heavily patronised; providing volunteers could be found, extras ran to Erith to help out the service 'buses. There was one Monday to Friday morning journey that turned at Villacourt Road – this was a bit of a performance as the frog handle had to be pulled in Wickham Lane with the 696 having to quickly get into Villacourt Road to avoid holding up traffic. I then had to run across the road and jump on the 'bus which turned round a large green in a small housing estate.

At Bexleyheath depot women conductors were deemed responsible for dealing with trolley arms (this was in contrast to all other depots where generally the men carried out this heavy work). I got a bit of a surprise one day when my driver said "Put the poles up Jean". It was always wise to check before leaving the depot that a bamboo stick was being carried; it was also worth making sure it was a long one because sometimes the poles would go high in the air when they came off. Sometimes the hook at the top of the bamboo stuck out of the end of the pole carrier – it had to be pushed or kicked back in. I had to guard my bamboo because though I'd check at the start of the shift to see I had one, I might find that if I left the 'bus for a cup of tea, someone would take my bamboo. I would only find this out when our poles came off the wires. Mind you, I was not averse to swiping someone else's pole! Bamboo poles would sometimes be seen hanging on traction poles and I would take one if I knew there wasn't one underneath. The maintenance men would sometimes get new supplies; despite that there were never enough to go round. They tended to 'disappear' but nobody knew what happened to them – it was if they were spirited away! One day my driver dewired going through Villacourt Road crossing and the poles were in a right state – both almost in the shape of an 'S'. It was a struggle to get them back on the wires but they just about fitted. Although the 696 could still move it came to a standstill in Woolwich as a policeman on traffic duty stopped us and told us to take the poles down on Parsons Hill stand as he considered the 696 to be unroadworthy. The 'bus had to be towed in; I was very annoyed as it was our last journey and I had a date after work – which was lost! I got very upset one day. It is a well-known fact that trolleybus staff had a billy can; this was filled with tea at certain cafes on the routes and we drank it when we were on stand time at a terminus. One day I picked up the can of tea at the Elite café at Erith but my driver went off before I boarded. I suppose he thought I was on and just kept going without the bell; I had to get on the next 698 but we didn't catch him up until Abbey Wood when he must have realised I wasn't on board. I cried and cried and cried and threw his tea in the road.

Crayford gets flooded from time to time. On 3rd September 1958 I was on early turn and waiting for the staff trolleybus; there had been torrential rain overnight and the River Cray had burst its banks. The flooding was so bad that the 'bus didn't come so I walked through the water to reach dry land. I was met by a gold badge inspector who frightened me to death by telling me I could have fallen down a sewer as all the manhole covers were up. The Cray hadn't flooded for sixty-one years but it decided to do so when I was on an early turn! Eventually I got to work. Trolleybuses started to go through to Dartford but had to run through water. We kept getting electric shocks so we turned at Bourne Road, and Country Buses on route 480 carried people from there. I had to do some downing and upping of booms as the trolleybuses had to turn on their batteries. Some vehicles got their motors damaged and London Transport dragged a few withdrawn ones from Fulwell to cover the shortage. They were dirty so our cleaners had to spend some time sprucing them up; they were with us for about ten days and went back in a better condition than they came! From the time I started until the end of the trolleybuses there always seemed to be some vehicles dumped at the back of the depot. There were some very early starts with Duty Two signing on at 4.15 am. The staff 'bus didn't leave Dartford until 4.31 to arrive at Bexleyheath Market Place at 4.48, meaning I couldn't get in on the very early shifts. Therefore I used my bicycle for duties starting before 5am. In thick fog I walked in front of the 'bus on occasions; this was scary at times. During foggy times I remember standing at Bexleyheath Clock Tower for hours on end waiting to relieve crews on their breaks. Staff trolleybuses ran each night. On Mondays to Fridays BX3/698 left Woolwich at 11.30pm showing Dartford Market Street. By the time it got to the depot most duties had finished; it would take on staff who wanted to go in the Dartford or Welling directions. When it got to Bexleyheath Market Place at 12.14am it became a staff journey. It arrived at Dartford at 12.31am, left at 12.37 for arrival at the depot at 12.59. Occasionally it might take home someone from Dartford Country bus garage.

> **Floods—Trolleybuses** 145
>
> On several occasions lately trolleybuses have been driven through flooded areas with disastrous results to motors, resulting in many vehicles being out of service for several days.
>
> The attention of staff is therefore again drawn to the instruction previously issued on this subject:
>
> "Trolleybuses must not be driven through floods when the depth of water is above the bottom edge of the side-guard slat. In all cases when driving through floods the speed must not exceed **WALKING PACE**, and trolleybuses should be kept as near to the **CROWN OF THE ROAD** as possible."

The honour of being the last trolleybus to leave the Kentish town of Dartford goes to 412B which worked in as a 698 from Woolwich. Normally the 698 stopped at Bexleyheath but this is a staff 'bus journey to accommodate drivers and conductors. BX3 awaits departure time. The heavily used wires glisten; in a day or two they will start to lose their lustre. *Charles Topham*

Duty One each day was an 'all-nighter'; we came in about 10pm each night. On Mondays to Fridays we'd take over BX 38 in Bexleyheath Market Place on the way to Woolwich on the 696; it left Woolwich at 11.07pm for Dartford as the last through journey. It left Dartford at 11.56, showing Plumstead Station, to arrive at Bexleyheath Market Place at 12.13 where it too became a staff journey. Both 'buses arrived at the Market Place simultaneously; excellent scheduling to accommodate drivers and conductors. Staff who had boarded BX3 could change and get the 696 to Welling and beyond. Passengers 'in the know' could also ride and pay a fare. BX 38 picked up staff at Plumstead garage before reversing at Plumstead Station. Leaving there, as a 698, more staff got on by Abbey Wood bus garage; they'd be dropped off through Erith and Barnehurst before arrival at Bexleyheath Market Place. Back to the depot for 1.26am - definitely no riders on this short run. Having a break we left the depot at 3.10am as a 696 to Plumstead. With just one minute stand it left for Dartford where it arrived at 4.27am to depart at 4.31am for Welling Corner. A few minutes there and to Dartford again where the staff 'bus element finished. We came off at Bexleyheath Market Place at about 5.30am; back to the depot to pay in which wasn't very much.

When the conversion to buses came there was not a farewell party; the trolleybuses came in on Tuesday night 3rd March 1959 and were parked up at the back, side and front of the depot. Next day everybody went out on buses as if nothing had changed. I was issued with a badge for RT buses - N59540. My dad had N59541. Now here's the thing. During the fourteen stage trolleybuses conversion programme was there any other instance of a father and daughter getting consecutive badge numbers? The Public Carriage Office issued all Bexleyheath conductors' badges in alphabetical name order; I had to pay out for another licence.

VEHICLE TIME CARD

ROUTES 696/
DARTFORD AND WOOLWICH (Powis Street) via WELLING,
BEXLEY AND WOOLWICH (Powis Street) via ERITH

TIME SCHEDULE NUMBER...........
OPERATING ON 6-5-56   LEAVE DEPOT 3-27   RUNNING NUMBER BX 12

Dartford	Princes Road	Bexley	Wheatley Arms	Walnut Tree Road	Welling Corner	Abbey Wood	Plumstead Station	Woolwich Powis Street Arrive	Woolwich Powis Street Leave	Plumstead Station	Abbey Wood	Welling Corner	Walnut Tree Road	Wheatley Arms	Bexley	Princes Road	Dartford
	*3-32	3-45			3-59	4-9				4-11		4-23			4-32	4-41	4-49
4-55	5-12		5-21									5-23			5-32 DEPOT	5-37*	
DEPOT 9-57																	
		10-2			10-11			10-31	10-33			10-53			11-2		
		11-6			11-15			11-35	11-37			11-57			12-6		
		12-12			12-21			12-41	12-43			1-3			1-12		
		1-16			1-25			1-45	1-47			2-7			2-16	2-25	2-33
2-38	2-46	2-55			3-4			3-24	3-26			3-46			3-55	4-4	4-12
4-18	4-26	4-35			4-44			5-4	5-6			5-26			5-35	5-44	5-52
5-58	6-6	6-15			6-24			6-44	6-46			7-6			7-15	7-24	7-32
7-38	7-46	7-55			8-4			8-24	8-26			8-46			8-55	9-4	9-12
9-18	9-26	9-35			9-44			10-1	10-6			10-26			10-35	10-44	10-52
10-58	11-6	11-15			11-24							11-26			11-35		
															DEPOT	11-40	

Sunday timecard which embraced the second half of the 'nighter'; this staff trolleybus duty finished at 5.37am - lovely.

The Chairman (Sir John Elliot) came to Bexleyheath Garage on Wednesday 4th March 1959. The reason for his attendance was to meet the crew of the first bus of the trolleybus changeover. This view was taken either on their relief or at the end of their shift. Our RT was out before the first Carshalton RT, hence him visiting us rather than them. Trolleybuses left to right are 415B, 390B and 97C which all show BEXLEYHEATH DEPOT; the 229 is RT 3927 (not the first vehicle, just one brought out for the picture). I recognise some of my colleagues. Far left is conductor Jack Stanley who is next to conductress Dot Carter. Two ladies along is Mrs Butler with Alan Duff next to her. Second from right is Eileen Evesson with Ron Hooper to her left. First crew out (at 4.15am) were driver Francis Lugg and conductor Albert Wade who are to the Chairman's immediate left.

London Transport Magazine

Eight of our trolleybuses were transferred to Walthamstow depot after we had finished with them. One was 798 which is just leaving the Crooked Billet terminus of route 685. There were a number of trips that only ran between Walthamstow Crooked Billet and Leyton Downsell Road on this route. As can be seen, a 'lazy' display has been provided (this showed both destinations on the same panel). This was at the request of the TGW union as the two destination panels for these places were a long way apart on the Walthamstow blind. By using the 'lazy' display a lot of aching arms were avoided. 798 looks smart so the Walthamstow cleaners are looking after her.

Fred Ivey

A forlorn sight at Penhall Road. 407B will last longer than most of the other trolleybuses here as it is being used as an office; the only other vehicle identifiable is 480. The trolleybus on the right is in a very mangled state, with the body having been pulled off the chassis. In the foreground are wheels and axles and other trolleybus paraphernalia.

Central Press Photos

As stated in her story, Jean came into contact with trams in her early years. The opportunity is taken to show a couple of photos in her childhood era and area.

Through some of Bostall Hill, trams had to work single line. This is shown by car ex-West Ham 299 which heads for EMBANKMENT on route 38 on the last day trams ran in London – 5th July 1952. Note that the car has its trolley arm on the positive trolleybus wire which is the means of electrical pick-up here. *Peter Mitchell 4104*

Former West Ham car 302 is in Woolwich High Street by Nile Street heading for Abbey Wood on route 36 on 7th October 1951. It is coming up to the change pit where it will shoot its plough and carry on from there by overhead. However, because Woolwich could become very tram-congested, overhead was strung further back than normal when approaching the plough-shift. The trolley pole has been placed on the overhead and the photographer has caught the trolley wheel sparking. This is because it is almost at the start of this facility and few trams take up the option this far back. Note the number of advertisements on the building to the left. The trolleybus overhead is for routes 696 and 698 so I passed here daily. *Peter Mitchell 2825*

799B again but only the bottom half! Presumably the roof bit being lifted by a crane at Penhall Road is 799B's. To think that I conducted this vehicle for a couple of years of my working life. On the right are six trolleybuses which haven't been touched by the scrapmen yet; it won't be long before breaking up equipment is taken to them and they are reduced to scrap. The handwritten '799B' was chalked on by London Transport at overhaul.
The 600 Group

A dozen of our trolleybuses were dismantled at Colindale; one was 424 which was delivered as a spanking new vehicle in 1936. Twenty three years later and after a lifetime of service to London's travelling public this is all that remains of her.
John L. Smith

Carshalton was first to change over as their last vehicle arrived about an hour before ours. Final trip from Dartford (and of a London trolleybus in Kent) was 412C with Mr A.S. Boney as driver and Kathleen Duffield as conductress. Last one into the depot was 405B which had been the staff trolleybus round Plumstead and Abbey Wood; when it reversed into Griffin Road it was the last use of a reversing triangle on the London trolleybus system. 405B was definitely last in. On the second half of the night duty an RT bus went out with the conductor having an easy time just ringing the bell. From the next night it was just one staff bus which was driver only.

Bexleyheath and Carshalton depots were involved in the first stage. There were big changes which involved a lot of route learning for drivers and conductors; a motorbus and driver was provided and it went out at various times in the days preceding the conversion so everybody would know where they were going and what they would be doing. The 696 was replaced by bus route 96 that had weekday peak hour journeys to Victoria Way, Charlton - an extension beyond the trolleybus terminus. The fare stages were from 99 down to 95 as Parsons Hill kept fare stage one as in trolleybus days. The 698 was replaced by the 229 which was extended from Bexleyheath depot to Woolwich with Monday to Friday peak hour trips to Victoria Way too. It now became Orpington Station to Woolwich and was worked jointly with Sidcup garage. We were way off our 'trolleybus beat' at Orpington. New route 195 went from Eltham to Woolwich in a very long-winded way; the 96 and 195 paralleled each other between Bexleyheath and Woolwich.

On Wednesday 4th March 1959 I was on early turn; everything looked different at the garage as it now was. Shiny RTs inside the building and trolleybuses parked outside. Cohen's, who bought the London trolleybuses for scrap, started taking them away that morning – twelve went to Colindale by Friday by which time eight had been towed to Walthamstow for more service. That freed up space. All trolleybuses had gone by mid-April – I saw many of them go; they were towed along the old 696 route and ended up behind Colindale depot or at a yard at Penhall Road Charlton where hundreds of London's trams had been burnt some years earlier. The overhead wires took longer to cut down. Trolleybuses seated seventy, RTs fifty-six. On the first days it was awful as there weren't nearly enough buses and consequently enough seats. On the second day I didn't know how many people had crammed on at Woolwich and they were standing on the staircase and upstairs. My driver came round and asked how many were on because the bus wouldn't move; we had to get some of them off to get going. London Transport had vastly under-estimated the number of seats required on the new routes. It was hard work on trolleybuses but was all good fun.

I'd always assumed that all of Bexleyheath's trolleybuses had been broken up for scrap. It is only with my involvement with the compilation of this book that I have found out that one survived. In 1959, the Paris Transport Museum contacted London Transport and asked if they would be prepared to donate a trolleybus to them; this was agreed. By now 796 was at Walthamstow depot; their foreman was instructed to find a good one and he chose 796 which sailed to France on 8th October 1960. The author of this book negotiated a deal for 796 to return to Britain which it did 49 years and 362 days later. It is on loan to the London Trolleybus Preservation Society and operates at the East Anglia Transport Museum where 796 is seen fully restored. *Frances Cui*

Colour Section

75 was one of thirty short-wheelbase B1 class trolleybuses allocated to Carshalton depot. Apart from odd sorties on the southern end of route 630 and trips to Fulwell overhaul works it would not have operated anywhere else other than between Sutton Green and Crystal Palace. On the forecourt 75 is ready for another trip on route 654. A facing frog, a trailing frog and a power feeder show up well in the winter sunshine. Time will soon be up for number 75 as builders' materials indicate the forthcoming change of occupants here.
Marcus Eavis, courtesy Online Transport Archive

B1 78 is parked on the traverser/turntable in Carshalton depot; soon it will be spun round to face the other way. Over the pits is 82 which is alongside the breakdown truck. It will not be long before the building loses its status as a trolleybus depot; contractors still have a fair amount of work to carry out before that occurs. *Terry Russell*

D2 440 is parked up outside Bexleyheath depot; it has no running number so is not allocated for service on Sunday 1st March 1959. The yellow poster in the nearside window details the forthcoming changeover of trolleybuses to motorbuses the following Wednesday. *Phil Tatt, courtesy Online Transport Archive.*

D2 456 leaves Hammersmith depot on route 630; the conductor is at the top of the front deck changing the destination blind; it looks as if 456 may just have come back from overhaul. At present, trolleybuses leave directly into Great Church Lane; before long they will have to brave fast-moving dual carriageway traffic to take up service.

Roy Hubble

In later years it was not an easy manoeuvre for trolleybuses leaving Hammersmith depot; they had to cross a dual carriageway with fast-moving traffic. A number of vehicles are inside the building waiting for their next call of duty. The signage on the building reads: LONDON TRANSPORT HAMMERSMITH TROLLEY. It should state: LONDON TRANSPORT HAMMERSMITH TROLLEYBUS DEPOT. Gusts of wind combined with a lack of maintenance?

John Laker

Q1 1819 is working on the 601 to Tolworth and outside the Stanley Road entrance of Fulwell depot. It was one of 125 trolleybuses exported to Spain in 1961; there she became La Coruna 25 and plied the streets of that city far longer than on the highways of her native London. This was the third of twenty-nine vehicles obtained by La Coruna that were converted for passengers to board on the right. Initially four of them, including number 25, had an open platform; this did not last long and they were soon altered to have a separate entry and exit. *John Laker*

To have regular access to London trolleybus depots, enthusiasts had to gain the trust of the engineers; the photographer was able to do this at a number of locations. Fulwell and Isleworth were not on his radar initially as it was anticipated that they would last until the late 1960s. However, the announcement that the Q1s were going to Spain in 1961 changed some of his priorities and in January of that year he was often seen in Fulwell depot. One occasion was 9th November 1961 when the engineers kindly brought out 1527 for him to take a final photograph of it under the wires; they had not got round to taking the blinds out. A massive change of vehicles occurred at stage twelve of the conversion scheme when many worn-out ex Highgate vehicles (1527 was one) were replaced by some well-maintained trolleybuses from Finchley depot. 1527 last ran on 7th November - on route 604.

Tony Belton

Fulwell's Q1s were replaced by L3s at stages nine and ten of the conversion programme; the incomers at stage nine came from Highgate of which 1401 is an example. It is working on route 667 and outside the maze of overhead in front of the Wellington Road end of the depot. *John Laker*

When trolleybuses needed to get from the Stanley Road end of Fulwell depot to the Wellington Road entrance, they had to use the link wire by the Nelson pub at Fulwell Junction; this is what is happening with 1494. The fact that it shows PRIVATE and has a blank side display indicates that this is an out of service journey.
Tony Belton

It must be a Sunday as this was the only time that trolleybuses would be seen parked up in the west side of Isleworth depot during daytime. At the head of a trio of vehicles is K1 1118. The water on the floor implies that maintenance staff have recently washed a vehicle. *Geoff McKenzie*

PULLING OUT OF ISLEWORTH. 1077 was immediately recognisable as it was the only trolleybus in the depot to have a Charlton produced blind – that was the front route number. This brilliant photograph shows 1077 leaving for Brentford Half Acre on route 657; it is picking up late for some reason as IH4 was not a scheduled 'swinger'. *Fred Ivey*

There were a number of turning points where facing frogs were not provided; the one at the bottom of Hillingdon Hill was used more prolifically than any other and was due to regular late running on route 607. On a bright summer's day F1 706 is having its trolley poles moved from the main line to the dead-ender at the bottom of Hillingdon Hill. These views clearly show the erroneous blind display of HILLINGDON CHURCH AND STRATFORD BDG. *John Laker*

Parked up in Hanwell depot, a number of trolleybuses are not in use. One is 1768 which London Transport will chose to represent its post-war style of trolleybus in their museum collection. Another Q1 is 1860 which is recently back from overhaul; it will remain stored and gather dust until the beginning of November 1960 when it will again show its paces on route 607 – albeit for just a few days. It will start working again at Fulwell on 9th November, continuing to operate there until 31st January 1961. It will then be exported to Spain and operate with the San Sebastian Tramways Company for many years. Also out of service is F1 737 – a number of workers' cars are also in view.
John Laker

From early morning until late evening there always seemed to be trolleybuses parked on Hanwell depot forecourt; this view exemplifies this. F1 668 is currently out of service; Q1 1845 is about to take up on route 607 to Hayes End Road while 712, one of a few F1s to retain a wire grille throughout its life, will soon be off to Clapham Junction on the 655. A bamboo pole hangs on a traction pole; this is handy as staff do not need to bend down to get one out from beneath a vehicle. London Transport publicity is prominent on the depot wall. A driver waits for his charge to turn up; crews would often congregate here to take up westwards. It is the summer of 1960; the date is ascertained by builders' materials – the building will not be known as Hanwell trolleybus depot much longer.
John Laker